AN ENCOURAGER
IS WITHIN YOU

Sis Wright
Thank you for your
support. Love ya!

AN ENCOURAGER
IS WITHIN YOU

DEBORAH HAMM

TATE PUBLISHING
AND ENTERPRISES, LLC

This book is designed to provide accurate and authoritative information with regard to the subject matter covered. This information is given with the understanding that neither the author nor Tate Publishing, LLC is engaged in rendering legal, professional advice. Since the details of your situation are fact dependent, you should additionally seek the services of a competent professional.

The opinions expressed by the author are not necessarily those of Tate Publishing, LLC.

Published by Tate Publishing & Enterprises, LLC
127 E. Trade Center Terrace | Mustang, Oklahoma 73064 USA
1.888.361.9473 | www.tatepublishing.com

Tate Publishing is committed to excellence in the publishing industry. The company reflects the philosophy established by the founders, based on Psalm 68:11,
"The Lord gave the word and great was the company of those who published it."

Book design copyright © 2015 by Tate Publishing, LLC. All rights reserved.
Cover design by Ivan Charlem Igot
Interior design by Gram Telen

Published in the United States of America

ISBN: 978-1-68142-311-1
1. Religion / Christian Life / Devotional
2. Self-Help / Spiritual
15.06.15

Acknowledgments

Special thanks given to my Lord and Savior Jesus Christ for placing in my heart the words to place on paper.

I would also like to thank my husband, Randall Hamm, for his patience, love, and support during this process.

Thank you to our grandchildren, Keon D. Clardy II and Jacob A. Clardy; our son and daughter-in-law, Keon D. Clardy and Samantha L. Clardy respectively; my parents, Rev. Clark Woodard (Emeritus) and Evangelist Mary A. Woodard, RN, who taught me how to hold onto God's unchanging hand despite the challenges life may throw at you;

And special thanks to Virginia Reams, author of *Words to Live By*; and Theresa Woodard, author of *Life in the Spirit*; Mimi Banford, CEO of MLB Sports & Entertainment; Pamela Benton; and the many others for your words of encouragement and prayers. Also, thank you to Dr. Ephraim Williams, pastor for your uncompromising words of guidance and Minister Perseus Poku Founder of AYCE Apologetics for your knowledge and support.

To the memory of Russell "Rusty" Hamm

To me Rusty was a man who, in spite of life challenges, smiled and cheered you up with honest words of wisdom, love, and hope.

He was diagnosed at an early age with Sickle Cell. Doctors said he would not live pass eighteen years of age. Rusty lived to be sixty years old. He loved music, cars and was an awesome artist!

Whenever, he would call and I answered the phone, he would say, "Hey, how is my girl?" You could just feel the smile through the phone. Even on days when he was not feeling well, he would give words of encouragement to Randall and say I am alright.

Three days before the Lord called him home, he was in the hospital in ICU. We were able to briefly speak to him over the phone and he said "Don't worry about me, I am alright."

I pray the words in this book encourage at least one soul to realize your value in God's eyes. Too many times, our focus is on man's opinions, man's ways, and man's thoughts to define our worth.

After reading this book, I charge each reader to look within yourself and during those times of grief, doubt, low self-esteem, feeling unappreciated, frustrated, or just needing guidance and comfort, look to the encourager within you who is the Holy Spirit to lift you up.

While people are active in discouraging you, the Holy Spirit is active in encouraging you. While people are trying to drag you down, the Holy Spirit is working to lift you up. While people are trying to get you to quit, the Holy Spirit is working to encourage you to finish.

Contents

Preface

Alexander Graham Bell wrote, "When one door closes, another door opens, but we so often look so long and so regretfully upon the closed door that we do not see the ones which open for us."

Have you ever given your best only to feel it is never good enough? Have you ever been overlooked because you are quiet? Have you ever been made to feel unappreciated and like your words are spoken to the wind? Lastly, have you been given a vision that others have watered down and made into the opposite of your vision only to make you feel less passionate about a project?

Have you ever thought about some of the causes of a person being discouraged? Unfortunately, some people become discouraged from trying so hard to please some people. Stop for one moment and ask yourself, why are you trying so hard to please this person/s? Is the outcome beneficial? Who is the outcome beneficial for? Is the focus of your vision spiritually based or secularly based?

Well, for one moment reread the quote by Alexander Graham Bell, and answer this question: Am I losing hope because of me, or am I allowing others to define me?

When I read this quote, I immediately had a flashback of my life. So many years I've dreamed of becoming a successful, highly sought-after international motivational speaker. Time after time, I started implementing steps toward achieving my goal only to stop. Some reasons for stopping were lack of finances, not feeling worthy, lack of connections, lack of transportation, lack of time, and the list goes on and on. The key words being *lack of*.

Well, it was one thirty in the morning. I was lying down, watching TV, or should I say the TV was watching me, feeling restless and frustrated. Wow, what a terrible combination. I briefly spoke to God and said, "Lord, I am tired. I've reached the end of my last rope. I do not know what to do anymore. What do you want me to do? I feel like I am not accomplishing anything."

The Lord spoke to me in a calm whisper, "Your biggest encourager is inside of you." This is how this book begins!

The Command

Each Christian has been given a command to admonish the idle, encourage the fainthearted, help the weak, and be patient with them all (1 Thess. 5:14). Christians have also been given the command to walk in a manner worthy of God, who calls you into his own kingdom and glory (1 Thess. 2:12).

Today's society is so consumed with leadership positions, social networking, and the different methodologies of getting a point across. Unfortunately, the lack of person to person communication and building relationships appears that some have forgotten or simply neglected how to extend encouragement, help, patience, and walk in a manner worthy of God.

Within the church, we have people in ministry leadership roles who have been there so many years until they feel entitlement and ownership to the point they are not willing to change. In some cases, they are not even open to change and are threatened by anyone who represents change in any format.

The downside is this attitude can become a hindrance toward the growth and/or self-esteem of a person who inwardly is struggling with personal challenges. It is not as easy as some make it seem to go to someone and discuss a problem you are having. Why? Could it be because humanity is losing its flavor of humility, confidentiality, integrity, and patience? Could it be these attributes are being replaced with deaf ears and negative attitudes?

Please, do not misunderstand the above statement. I am only speaking on a select few things that may cause a person to feel discouraged. What I am saying is sometimes, the challenges people are facing are deeply rooted in connection to a mental, physical, or emotional state. Some problems may need counseling, medication, or just a listening, nonjudgmental ear. When a person is reaching out, try to be attentive to him or her. When the response is given with an uncaring, low dry tone, and very little eye contact, it can leave an unpleasant conclusion. When you project a less-than-attentive tone, body behavior, or appearance, it may place a confusing or even an apathetic effect with the person. For a person to rise above the challenges of negativity, a person needs to hear or at least see something positive from you. You never know, this person may be praying all the time and just need a sensitive, humble listening ear and some assistance with direction. Depending on their individual response, their tone, their body language, and their personal level of faith or spiritual maturity, this type of response can send a person a few steps backward, not to mention depending upon who is the responder. We are called to build each other up not tear each other down.

"And let us consider and give attentive, continuous care to watching over one another, studying how we may stir up (stimulate and incite) to love and helpful deeds and noble, activities, Not forsaking or neglecting to assemble together (as believers) as is the habit of some people, but admonishing (warning, urging, and encouraging) one another, and all the more faithfully as you see the day approaching…" (Hebrews 10:24-25 Amplified Version).

Could it be people who have no clue what it means to love are giving advice on how to love? Could it be people who have no sympathy or empathy are the ones sent to give comfort to others or voluntarily the ones giving comfort? Could it be people in some leadership positions are not leading according to God's word? Could it be people who will not move or step down are mentoring others and are not doing any of the things mentioned in the book of Titus about training and mentoring others? Could it be people are meeting the needs of others according to what they think and not the real needs of the people? Could it be leadership roles are following the family tradition instead of the biblical foundation? You know where every member in the family holds a position in the church. Half are awesome with their roles and responsibilities. Others are just wearing a title.

Although, each Christian is to help and encourage each other, the encourager with the most impact should be the encourager within you. The question is what spirit is within you? The spirit I am speaking of is The Holy Spirit. This spirit takes up residence when you give your life to Christ. This encourager is the Holy Spirit.

Note: While people are active in discouraging you, the Holy Spirit is active in encouraging you. While people are trying to drag you down, the Holy Spirit is working to lift you up. While people are trying to get you to quit, the Holy Spirit is working to encourage you to finish.

When you find yourself needing a word of encouragement and no one is around, remember God is always near. The Bible says, "God has said, Never will I leave you; never will I forsake you" (Hebrews 13:5 NIV).

Take a moment and think on these words: We are living in a society that brings to our awareness on a daily basis the trouble and strife in this world. It is written in the Bible, "I have told you these things, so that in me you may have peace. In this world you will have trouble. But take heart! I have overcome the world" (John 16:33 NIV). "Everywhere you go, there is trouble and strife. But God is standing by!"

Pray and ask God what to do in every decision of your life. God may place a scripture in your mind or remind you of a similar situation. He may even send someone to you or even have someone to call you. God works in ways unknown to us, but I know He is always on time when He answers.

Expect and answer from the Lord. Always keep a notebook to write down what the encourager within you places on your heart. Write your thoughts immediately because you may forget them later.

Write it down. Writing out your thoughts, scriptures, etc. exposes lazy thinking. Pray that God will enable you to "be submissive" unto the leading of the Holy Spirit. Prayer is the key to the Kingdom. Prayer is communicating or talking to God.

Meditate. This involves reading. Reread and reread. Be certain you understand what the passage/scripture means. Pray for God to supply and bless, especially when you are experiencing challenges within your life.

Pray to maintain your focus. All your decisions should reflect the answers God has given you. Rely on the lead of the encourager within you.

Let's take a brief journey with a young lady named Tatiana and her encourager named Grace.

Snoozing

Tatiana loved socializing. In her eyes, nothing could go on without her or her insight. She was an intelligent, beautiful, successful young lady, who was financially well off and a graduate from a very prestigious university.

In others' eyes, Tatiana has the perfect life. She is the wife of a handsome, attentive, wealthy man, she has two children (a boy and a girl), owns her home, and drives a BMW and a Mercedes. What more could a girl ask for? Well, she just found out their home was in foreclosure, and her husband wants a divorce. Looking at how her life just spun upside down, she dare tell anyone. After all, she is a diva!

She was very active in her church, pretending all is well. She maintained her busy schedule until one day, she went into a depression. Her associates said she was crazy and tripping. After all, they enjoyed hanging out with her. Probably because they never had to contribute anything, she always took care of her so-called friends. You know, she had a reputation to uphold.

Once per month, Tatiana visited the nursing home for her monthly community service as she called it. There was one lady who she admired by the name of Maggie. They called her "Grace." She had silky, shiny silver streaks in her hair, and she was quiet yet graceful in everything she did.

Grace was always happy to see Tatiana. This one particular Wednesday, she saw Tatiana coming from a distance, looking a little perplexed. Grace stated, "Sweetie, what's the problem? You appear a tad bit perplexed."

Tatiana replied with a smile, "Oh, you know the usual. Just have a lot on my plate."

"Well, Tatiana," replied Grace, "time is too short, and you are too young to have so much on your plate that you look the way you're looking today. Are you tired of trying to please all the people you socialize with? As a matter of fact, why do you spend so much of your time trying to please everybody? Baby, do you know over half those people do not really have your best at heart. My mother told me as a child to watch out for those who stick to you when the good rolls around. Because, baby, when the bad takes its turn, you will not find them.

Tatiana looked at Grace with a half smile and replied, "Not my girls. I am very careful. All I socialize with is people in the church. You know, occasionally, with a coworker or two. I am active in my church, and they are always calling on me. I have a reputation to uphold. The titles I have alone are prestigious! I am a born leader. People know it, and I represent it well.

"That's fine, baby, but whom and how do you represent? Is it arrogantly, humbly? How? I tell you what, while you brush my hair, let me share a story with you.

"There was a woman in the Bible named Deborah. Her name meant 'honey bee.' Her greatest accomplishment was that she led Israel as a prophet and judge. Deborah was charming. She had an intimate relationship with God. When she spoke for God, she gave it her all (Judg. 5:31).

"During the time of oppression, the Israelites were dominated by the Philistines. Now Deborah was humble and listened to God. Deborah gained respect from the Israelites not because of her beauty. She as you say 'represented' well. Her focus was on God. She was a wife (Lapidoth), and her husband had a prestigious title as judge (Judg. 4:4).

"Even though Deborah's focus was on what God desired of her. She never thought nothing could go on without her or her insight, nor assumed the Israelites felt this way. Her role as a wife and a leader was never to the point where she said, 'I have a lot on my plate.'

Baby, I hope you don't mind me calling you baby? If you do, you'll get over it (Grace, smiles). Let me explain who Deborah is by using the acronym RESPECT "Deborah. respected herself and others with whom she worked, exceeded the expectations of others, stood firm on her convictions, possessed uncommon sense of security and maturity, experienced personal success, contributed to the success of others, and thought ahead of others.

"I said all that to ask you, baby, do you respect yourself and others? It's time out for the 'I have arrived mentality.' It's time out for thinking just because you attend and are active in church that everything is peachy keen. It's time out for holding onto titles and material gain. It's time to wake up and serve the Lord!

"God is the person who has gifted you with your talents and gifts. He gave you those leadership roles. He gifted you for spiritual leadership. However, not every leadership role is appropriate for you. And no title gives anyone the right to assume the sun does not rise or set without them. No amount of money, degree, or prestige will get you to heaven. No matter how many ministries you are in, no human can or will give you a free ticket to heaven. Baby, don't let your success go to your head.

"You are an intelligent young lady. What are you doing in your life for the Lord? Are you more focused on the outer appearance, praise, and popularity vote from your peers and others? Do you go to church to socialize with church folks? Or do you go to worship with the saints! Baby, I mean WORSHIP the Lord. Study the Bible. Study about the virtuous woman. As a matter of fact, let's have Bible study every time you come see me. Can we do that?"

"Oh yes, I would love that, Grace. But we have to stop now. I'm energized and thinking now!"

"Yes, baby, you may be energized, but I'm tired. As a matter of fact, study the book of Ecclesiastes and that will be our discussion next month, 'A Time for Everything.' Go home and talk to the Lord. Learn to listen to Him. I said next month because I am going out of town to visit my daughter. I should be back in a couple of weeks. Then let's talk about if you woke up or are still snoozing."

"Uh, what does that mean, Grace?"

"Don't worry, you'll understand one day."

Grace started singing, "By and by when the morning comes, when the saints of God are gathered home, we'll tell the story how we've overcome; for we'll understand it better by and by"(Song Title: We'll Understand It Better By and By; by C. A. Tinley, Arranged by F.A. Clark. The New National Baptist Hymnal, page 325, copyright 1977).

As you are reading this book, what do you think about Grace and Tatiana's conversation?

_____

_____

_____

_____

_____

_____

_____

_____

_____

_____

_____

_____

_____

_____

_____

_____

_____

_____

_____

_____

_____

_____

_____

_____

_____

_____

_____

_____

_____

_____

_____

_____

_____

_____

After speaking with Grace, Tatiana realized that she was such a people pleaser. It was a shock to her because she always thought she had her life under control. It wasn't until she was down and wondering what was missing that she even started focusing on her life.

After speaking with Grace, she went home, spoke with her husband about their conversation, and for the first time, she picked up her Bible with a focused mind on receiving an understanding, not just to read. She asked God for wisdom and her purpose in life.

It wasn't until I started writing, teaching, and speaking more that I became more sensitive to my actions and words. Just like Tatiana, one day, I woke up and realized I was a people pleaser. I could feel myself wanting to scream. The good part is I didn't.

Now the shock is on the other person/s, for I am speaking out and up as the Holy Spirit leads me.

It is something when you are teaching a class and the finger is pointing back at you every time you teach. There have been times during my teaching and even speaking engagements, I would stop a second and think, *Wow, this lesson is speaking and teaching my life.* Well, as a teacher/speaker that's okay as long as you and I learn and grow from the lessons we teach or speak on.

I thank God for allowing me enough time to get it together. I have some work to do. I got to keep it real. So if you don't like it real as real can get, close the book now. I will not be mad at you. I don't live with you, and you are not accountable to me. But if you want to learn more about reality and what's happening right under your own eyes, keep reading and encourage someone else to read this book. Actually, you can even purchase one for someone as a gift.

Tatiana and Grace's Bible Study

"Grace, I hope you are ready. I've been reading, praying, and meditating. What made you pick the book of Ecclesiastes?"

"Well, good afternoon to you too. Did you enjoy your trip? How are you doing?" said Grace.

Tatiana replied, "Oh, I'm sorry. How are you doing today, Grace? I really missed you. How was your trip? Excuse my rudeness. I am excited! It's like something is stirred up inside me just waiting for our Bible lesson."

"Well, that's good and all. In response to your questions, all is good. But never forget to have class when starting a conversation. Remember the acronym RESPECT that we learned from the lifestyle of Deborah? Always remember that. Now that we have had our brief life application this morning, let's have prayer, a song, and start our lesson.

"Lord, thank you for your uncompromised word. Thank you for the fire that is stirred up in Tatiana to know you in a more intimate way. And, Lord, I thank you for one more day. Amen.

"Okay, young lady, what is your synopsis on Ecclesiastes?"

"Oh, Grace, it is good! I learned that I have been living wrong. I thought material things, attending church, having a good job, education, husband, children, you know the entire package, that all was good. I found out that I was like totally blind!"

"Well, sweetie, I wouldn't say you were totally blind, maybe a little." Grace laughed. "We all have or are experiencing blindness in our life in some area or areas. The solution as you are learning is in God's word. The enemy wants to keep you blind. `But Jesus came on the scene that we may see and live!"

"Grace, why did you choose the book of Ecclesiastes for this week?"

"Because when you came to see me the last time, it was all over your face that you didn't know what time it was. I mean you appeared perplexed and straight out lost. So I figured it was the perfect time to speak. All the other times you visited me, you would not have received what I had to offer because you were into yourself. The Lord let me know you were ready to listen now, and the keyword was *time*, and what better book to study on than a book that was dealing with time. So what did you learn?"

"I learned that it's not about me! You know I am cute and all." Tatiana smiled. "But it's not about me. I wasn't placing God first in my life. I was playing church. Oh, I was a 'church folk.' And my so-called friends were not! They were Jobs's friends' cousins because they are saying I am tripping and going through menopause or something—"

Grace interrupted, "Why are they saying that?"

"Because I am not spending as much time as I use to shopping, eating out, and you know doing the things we use to do. I am prioritizing my time. I even sit closer in church now because I don't want to miss anything. The book of Ecclesiastes taught me that there is a time for everything, and my season of selfishness is over. I didn't think I was pretending about anything. I was just tangled up in what the world considered successful and happy. I learned that God wants me to be happy and successful, and nothing is wrong with my accomplishment or status. He wants me focus on eternity and not a minute of self/manmade happiness."

Grace smiled and replied, "I believe somebody has been thinking and talking with the Lord while I was away. And you are correct. It is time out for playing church and thinking the sun rises and sets around what we want or think we should have. Well, I am a little tired, even though I am truly enjoying your visit. How about we study the book of John this time? I'll see you in another month," she replied, smiling.

They close out with a prayer and Grace begins singing, "Without God I could do nothing, without Him I would fail;

without Him my life would be rugged, like a ship without a sail." (Song Title: Without God I Could Do Nothing; by Beatrice Brown, Arranged by Kenneth Morris. The New National Baptist Hymnal, page 320, copyright 1977).

As you are reading this book, what do you think about Grace and Tatiana's conversation?

_____

_____

_____

_____

_____

_____

_____

_____

_____

_____

_____

_____

_____

_____

_____

_____

_____

_____

_____

_____

_____

_____

_____

_____

_____

_____

_____

_____

_____

_____

_____

_____

_____

_____

Be Real, and Stop Pretending

It's time out for pretending that some folks, and even in church are not straight out tripping! It's time out for pretending that some leaders and even in church do not need to be removed! It's time out for pretending that you are perfect! It's time out for pretending that each of us does not have our own share of issues! It's time out for pretending that you do not need to learn more about Jesus on a daily basis! It's time out for pretending that you do not need to read, study, and meditate on God's Word daily! It's time out for pretending that you do not need to pray every day. It's time out!

People of all nationalities are facing the economic challenges of this day and time. People are losing their homes, cars, lives, loved ones, 401Ks, investments, jobs, minds etc. People are in a state of disbelief, frustration, and depression. There is a lack of respect in places where you would not expect. Disrespect is rapid within the church, workplace, and homes. People are treated like they are not valued, appreciated, or even wanted. People are afraid to ask for help because it is shared in conversations with others.

And no matter how you share it, it always get back to the person, then the person is embarrassed, ashamed or just become a loner. This is sad!

This world is in chaos, and it will get worst if people including the people within the church don't get it together and stand for what is right according to God's Word. Leaders are the example whether you want to accept it or not. Therefore, if you can't be the positive example or role model for others as leaders, then step down. Stepping down doesn't mean you are a bad person. A person can step down and work on their people skills, develop their gifts, take some training courses, etc.

People are leaving the church and not being active within the church in some cases because they don't want to deal with the president, chairperson, cochairpersons, or some members within the ministry. This is not leading or being an effective witness according to God's Word. For in His Word it states, everything must be done in an orderly manner (1 Cor. 14:40). And God is not in the midst of confusion within the church body.

Learn the tricks of the enemy. Satan is in the midst of confusion and deception within the church. We all make mistakes and have good and bad days. However, people don't necessarily have to be sinful to be ineffective toward kingdom building. Satan loves it when the saints are confused about what God wants. He loves it when the saints are lukewarm. And, yes, he loves it when saints in leadership roles are arrogant, self-centered, and their mind far from what God wants! This creates a problematic ministry. And it can have a domino effect within the church if the leader of any ministry is in denial of their effects on the members of the ministry and if not addressed within a timely manner, properly and lovingly. Now, could this me you?

It's time out for thinking because of your title that you do not have to do kingdom building. It's time out for thinking to get attention you will say the Lord called you when you know He didn't. Keep it real!

When you accept a certain calling, there is much work to do. God does not call someone to ministry to sit down, stick out your chest, say a few words at annual day programs, or walk around to be seen. It's time out for perpetrating and procrastination, in the church.

I don't know about you, but the God I serve is in control. I must decrease that He may increase. In other words, humble myself and allow God to work in and through me that God receives the glory! God always has my back. Do you know of anyone who no matter what always has your back anytime of the day, several times per day? As long as I stop flipping (talking too much) and tripping and focus on what God wants me to do, it will work out for the good. You may not like it, but God is who we need to focus on pleasing, not ourselves.

One thing I have learned is a person focused on what God wants will not mistreat, belittle, or disrespect any person. For the God we serve will show and tell us how to handle all situations, and in the end, God has our back as long as we are obedient to this word.

Let's take a brief look at one person in the Bible who God had his back. The person chosen for this discussion is Joseph. For detailed information read Genesis 30-50.

Joseph, the favorite son of Jacob, had brothers who did not like him. On top of being the favorite son, he was confident, received a very special coat from his father, and he was a dreamer along with being an interpreter of dreams.

He was sold into slavery by his brothers. Not only was this confusing that his own flesh and blood was doing this; it was hurtful to Joseph. The last thing I could ever imagine is to be sold by family because of dislike or jealousy into slavery.

Once taken to Egypt, one of Pharaoh's officials bought him from the Israelites (Genesis 39:1). Joseph did not complain through this process. In spite of the circumstances, he did not remove his focus off God.

Favor of God was upon Joseph for he lived in his master's house, who later placed him in charge of everything. Unfortunately, the wife of his master tried to seduce Joseph. He did not take the bait and said no on more than several attempts that were made. The last attempt, he ran so fast out of the house that he left his cloak. This was the evidence used against him in the words of Potiphar's wife that led to his imprisonment (Genesis 39:2-20).

While imprisoned, he still found favor with the Lord through the warden who placed Joseph in charge of the inmates. Once again, Potiphar is at two other servants whom he has imprisoned in the same jail as Joseph. Through his interpretation of dreams for the cupbearer and the baker (who were the two other servants), God once again shows favor toward Joseph. Pharaoh is having dreams that cannot be interpreted, and Joseph is referred to him by the cupbearer. Once the dreams are successfully interpreted and Joseph is seen to have favor once more of God, Pharaoh now places him over the whole land of Egypt.

A little further in the life of Joseph, he is blessed with a wife and later two sons. After seven years of abundance, famine spreads over the country. Joseph opens the Egyptian storehouses and sells grain to the Egyptians. People come from miles and days away to purchase grain in Egypt. We have now reached full circle where Joseph's brothers show up in Egypt to purchase grain. They do not even recognize their own brother at this stage.

Joseph could have been extremely vindictive for what was done to him. Yet he rose over great adversity and was known as a very prominent person in Egypt. After a few testing given to his brothers, he reveals who he is and helps his family.

Whereas, what some people mean for bad, just keep your mind focused on God who has your back as long as you are obedient to him. He can turn your enemies, your obstacles, your low self-esteem, and your doubts around for the good.

Just as God had Joseph's back, in advance He arranged for Joseph to be the provider and survivor for his family. His brothers who sold him into slavery.? In the end, his obedience to God's plan, allowed Joseph without vengeance to take them in and supply their needs.

Grace and Tatiana's Third Visit

"Hi, Tatiana, how are you today? It is always a delight visiting with you. Before we begin, I just want to thank you for making time for an old lady like me. I'm sorry our visit has to be short today. So do you mind if we go ahead and pray?"

"No problem. Are you all right today?"

"Yes, just a little tired." She began praying, "Our Father who art in heaven, hollow will be thy name, thy kingdom come, thy will be done. Lord, thank you for this young lady who desires to know you more each day. Thank you for allowing an old lady like me to share with her about your goodness. Continue to walk with her. Carry her through the challenging times, laugh with her through the good times, cry with her in the sad times. But more than anything, walk with her in all times. Give her wisdom and understanding of your Word. Let her light shine brightly everywhere she goes. This is your servant's prayer in Jesus Name. Amen.

"Well, young lady, what's the lesson from the book of John?"

"Grace, I learned that only what you do for Christ will last. I don't know of anyone who would go through what Jesus went through for me. I don't know how much time I have, so I want to get it right. We are so blessed to have more than a second chance to get it right. I believed that Jesus is the Son of God and that He died and rose again. I believed when Jesus said, 'I am the way, the truth and the life; no one comes unto the Father but by me.'(John 14:6 NKJV) But now, I believe it within my heart not just verbally. Since I have been making more time in my life for God, I've noticed my girls no longer want to hang with me. But that is okay, I just pray for them. I still speak to them and will help if able.

Maybe when they see how happy I am inside, they will get on board! If not, I will continue to pray for them and live for Christ.

Tatiana sighed a little and said, "Thank you, Grace, for opening my eyes. I am investing in some resources to assist my growing and maturing in Christ."

Grace replied, "You're welcome, sweetie, but to God goes the glory! Now let's close out with prayer. Lord, thank you for your divine revelation. Thank you for the Holy

Spirit. Thank you for your comforting word. In Jesus name, Amen."

Grace ended as usual, singing, "Angels get my mansion ready, I am coming home/I am coming home to heaven, with the angels there to dwell, I am coming home to glory, where I'll never say farewell/I am coming to that city, nevermore to roam, Angels get my mansion ready, I am coming home." (Song Title: Angels Get My Mansion Ready; by C. Austin Miles. The New National Baptist Hymnal, page 435, copyright 1977).

As you are reading this book, what do you think about Grace and Tatiana's conversation?

_____

_____

_____

_____

_____

_____

_____

_____

_____

_____

_____

_____

_____

_____

_____

_____

_____

_____

_____

_____

_____

_____

_____

_____

_____

_____

_____

_____

_____

_____

_____

_____

_____

Accepting Is Only One Step

In the midst of accepting the Lord in our lives, we have a responsibility to seek knowledge, wisdom, and understanding. Why would you not want to know God on an intimate level? Well, could it be that you are held to a higher level of accountability? I can't speak for others since I don't know your life or lifestyle. I do know someone who knows everything about you, your thoughts, your actions, and your heart. Now knowing that someone knows the deepest, most inner thoughts of your life, wouldn't you want to know this person? The awesome part is God has made it available for everyone to know Him on a personal and intimate level.

God has given us more than enough resources to learn more about Him. He has given us in writing His promises and commandments to help us in this journey. He has given us more than enough resources to learn how to live a prosperous life. He has given us more than enough resources to learn how to deal with the challenges of this life. And yes, He has given us more than enough resources to reach all nationalities, ages, and gender of people. The key is within you. Why, do you not want to know your Father? Let's break it down a little more. People use the phrase, "Who's your daddy?" So I am going to say it in those terms; don't you want to know who your real daddy is?

I hope you don't mind if I just keep it real and to the point. I am writing to the church! You know the ones who are saved. I like to say the ones who have been signed, sealed, and delivered.

You know the ones who acknowledged the ABCs (Accept that Jesus Christ is Lord; Believe that He is the Son of God that He died and rose again; and Confessed with their mouth that we are sinners saved by grace.)

When you accepted Christ in your life, your work was just beginning. Time out, can you hear me now?

Can You Hear Me Now?

"Don't be scared." God has not given us the spirit of fear, but the spirit of power, of courage, and of resolution to meet difficulties and dangers. He has given us the spirit of love to God, which will carry us through opposition, and he has given us the spirit of sound mind. The Holy Spirit is not the author of a timid, cowardly disposition, and God is not the author of confusion. In the word of God, He informs us to do everything decent and in order (1 Cor. 14:40).

People will let you down. After all, when Paul was arrested in Asia Minor, no one came to see him (2 Tim. 1:15). When he was in Rome, he was locked up and kept out of circulation so it would be difficult to locate him. However, one man (Onesiphorus) was faithful until he found Paul (2 Tim. 1:16–17).

Paul informed Timothy that his motivation stood firm in the knowledge of the Lord and guidance of the Holy Spirit. He tells Timothy to be a good Christian soldier and gave him several key points.

1. Be a teacher of God's word.

2. Don't be consumed with worldly mess (Ro 12:2).

3. Endure hardships. Christ got your back if you are obedient (2 Tim. 2:3).

4. Study God's word.

5. Don't add to nor take away from his Word (Deut. 12:32).

6. Don't twist the scriptures (2 Pet. 3: 15–16).

7. Meditate (Ps. 1: 1–3).

8. Keep sound doctrine.

God gave us several commands. However, I will expound on only one, which was the Great Commission. "Go ye therefore and teach all nations" (Matt. 28: 19). This means we can have confidence when sharing the truth about Jesus to others because we have Jesus' divine authority to back it up. Our responsibility is to be faithful messengers; this is what Paul is explaining to Timothy. Don't worry about what others may say. You make sure your walk, talk, and actions exemplify Christ. Don't worry about what others think or say.

Some people out of negativity will always point at mistakes. *Excuse me, it is an honest mistake.* Focus on doing what God wants, if someone does not like you, oh well, remember everyone did not like Jesus and some still don't. Realize you are not perfect, and you will make some mistakes. You will fall down sometimes. But trust me, by the grace of God and with God's strength and guidance, you'll get back up! I'm getting up! And I will be stronger, wiser, better, and more passionate about the vision and mission assigned to me. For I am a vessel waiting to be used by God, And God can and will give me the power to deal with life challenges. God got the power, and I am tapping in!

Power. It is not for us to know how, where, when, and why something is going to happen before it happens. But it is for us to know God has given us power. His Word states,

> But ye shall receive Power, after that the Holy Ghost shall come upon you; and ye shall be my witness unto me both in Jerusalem, and in all Judea, and in Samaria and unto the uttermost part of the earth. (Acts 1:8)

As Christians, we are ambassadors, introducing people who don't know Jesus to the love and grace available at no cost to them. We are effective only through the power of the Holy Spirit. For all gifts that come from God to sinful man, come in and through Jesus only! "I am the way, the truth and the life no man comes unto the Father but by me" (John 14:6).

Paul admonishes Timothy and informs him that a good man will seek to do well. There are two things we must all do: (1) get real, and (2) grow up. Stop complaining about what others are not doing. For if they are truly striving to be more like Christ, they wouldn't show signs of confusion, laziness, gossiping, cliques, or selfishness. Some people are just not going to listen to you. That is all right, just keep doing what you do as long as it lines up with the word of God.

It's time out! Can't you hear God speaking through nature, diseases, the economy, people, and blessings, etc. If not, correct me if I'm wrong; you have attended or heard enough Easter services I'm sure. So through the sermons you heard, didn't you hear God speaking through Calvary?

It is because of Calvary and Jesus love for mankind that He sent unto us a comforter in the form of the Holy Spirit. When we became saved, we instantly became sealed, and the Holy Spirit took up residence within us. The Holy Spirit is not forceful. You have to permit the Holy Spirit to guide and instruct you (Matt. 10:19–20). Just as you need to know God the Father, and God the Son, you need to know who the Holy Spirit is!

The Bible promises us that the Holy Spirit will guide us. Jesus does not promise us that the Holy Spirit will control us or force us to do anything. At no point do we lose our ability to choose to follow His lead. Consequently, we are always responsible for our choices, words, and actions.

The Holy Spirit is a person who will guide all believers into all truth. (John 16:13). That means His guidance is trustworthy. As you develop greater sensitivity to His guidance, you will worry much less about the decisions you make.

The church's responsibility is to bring the inquirer to a clear and intelligent decision for Christ. We are to Confess (1 John 1:9); believe (Rom. 1:16); forgive (1 John 1:9); invitation (John 1:12); prayer (the sinner's prayer).

Now I can't assume everyone knows what I am talking about. Therefore, just in case you didn't attend the Easter service or hear of Jesus, below is a brief synopsis of a court case about Him. To learn more, read the Holy Bible. It comes in many versions. I prefer the King James Version, the New International Version, and the American Standard Version

----

Let's take a moment to discuss one of the most analyzed court cases. For the sake of this book, the case will be represented by a hypothetical law firm. We will name it the Trinity Law Firm.

This case is represented by the Trinity Law Firm, which is a universal firm licensed by the Creator, God the Father, responsible for the creation and salvation of sinners, hereby consents and joins in the adoption petition filed by the named petitioner, who is Jesus Christ.

Pursuant to the provisions of the family adoption code in 2 Corinthians 5:20, section 47 (New Testament), it is hereby stated that the condition of the persons who are the subject of this petition is: Sinners

Mediation was successfully used in the form of parables, examples, and unmatchable teachings through constant prayer, meditation, and devotions. It is hereby stated the petitioner in this case is certified. He is known as Immanuel, prince of peace, Anointed One, Son of God, Son of Man, Lamb of God, Christ, rabbi, alpha and omega, King of kings, Lord of lords, bright and morning star, Lion of Judah, etc.

The Trinity Law Firm has supplied documentation in the form of the Holy Bible to assist the respondents with their growth as adoptee in the spiritual family of kingdom building.

We acknowledge that sin is still a powerful force, but it can no longer control the respondents of this petition unless they allow it to do so. They are not doomed to failure, and to believe otherwise is to remain in needless, painful bondage. That breaks the heart of the Trinity Law Firm and grieves the spirit. Cross reference: "Do not grieve the Holy Spirit of God, with whom you were sealed for the day of redemption" (Eph. 4:30).

All who have changed their name from "sinner" to "saved" are truly blessed according to code Jeremiah 17, sections 7 to 8.

> Blessed is the man who trusts in the Lord, and whose hope is the Lord. For he shall be like a tree planted by the waters, Which spreads out its roots by the river,

And will not fear when heat comes; But its leaf will be green, And will not be anxious in the year of drought, Nor will cease from yielding fruit.

The Old Testament prophesied:

1. God will declare the messiah (Jesus) to be His Son (Ps. 2:72).

2. All things would be placed under the messiah's feet (Ps. 8:63).

3. God will forsake Him in His hour of need (Ps. 22: 1).

4. He will be mocked and insulted (Ps. 22:7–8).

5. His hands and feet will be pierced (Ps. 22:16).

6. He will be accused by ruthless witnesses (Ps. 35:11).

7. He will be hated without any reason (Ps. 35:19).

8. He will be betrayed by a friend (Ps. 41:9).

9. His throne will be forever (Ps. 45:6).

10. He will ascend to God's right hand (Ps.68:18).

According to God's Word (the Bible) all the above were fulfilled in the following passages:

- Matt. 3:17; Matt. 27:46;
- Mark 14:57; Mark 16:19;
- Luke 22:47; Luke 23:34–35;

- John 15:25; John 20:25, 27;
- Heb. 1:8; Heb. 2:8.

When a person accepts Christ in their life and are saved, he/she become adopted into the body and family of Christ.

This is the witness of God, which He hath testified of His Son in code 1 John section 5:6–11. Welcome to God's family of dedicated, baptized believers!

Who Has Your Attention

The life you live should show inwardly and outwardly. The words we say should articulate the truth. Commit yourself to speaking only what is right and true (James 8:6–8). In some cases, what you know as truth does not give you the right to speak on to others. This would especially be true when someone has confided in you. Don't spread their business around. This is also true when receiving third-party information. Go to the source. Ask the source, and stop relying so heavily on your cliques or people who appear to know it all. Trust me, no one but God knows it all.

Within the church, people are hurting and looking for comfort and help in many areas. This means confidentiality is a priority! If you can't trust here, where can you trust? Stop allowing others to bring negativity to you. If everyone did this, just imagine the effect the church could have on the community, government, marriages, youth, etc. When speaking the truth, be humble and loving (Eph. 4:29). Listen attentively before you speak (James 1:19). It is not wise to lie on someone or about someone for attention (Prov. 12:22). Our lifestyle should reflect a commitment to God. Stop feeling threatened by other people's gifts, talents, and skills.

Imagine for a moment you were a trash can (no disrespect intended here). You are clean on the outside, shining, and looking good. Now every few minute, you are approached with some person/s sharing gossip, lies, jealousy, envy, complaints, finger pointing, etc. This doesn't sound too appealing, does it? Well, that shining exterior becomes dull, and the odor is not that pleasant anymore. Get my drift. Just because of your title, how long you have been a member, how financially blessed you are, how materialistically blessed you are, does not make you the only expert on life, nor does it make you immune to self-evaluation and attitude adjustments if needed.

Well, there was a time when I was struggling with challenges and made several mistakes and bad decisions. To be exact, very recently, I went to sleep, and my conscience got the better half of me. This was because I knew I was wrong. I allowed my emotions to get the best of me because I was disappointed of the disrespect shown, and it hit home a little. After venting, I had to get on my knees and apologize to God, for the inner man and the outer man didn't match up. If you noticed, this entire paragraph has one keyword, *I*.

This is the problem. It's not about me, and it is not about you. It's all about God's kingdom. The "I" mentality can become a potential disaster, when your focus is on self-edification. When experiencing challenges, do a self-evaluation, and make sure you did not cause the problem or initiate a chain reaction of gossip that triggered the problem. Have you done this?

Spending more time with the Lord enables you to feel His presence and love more and more and more. As our lives are being transformed from the old self to the new self, it is called a "transitional change." Our conduct should reflect the life we now have in Christ, but never underestimate how the enemy is constantly searching for ways to remove your focus off God's plan for your life. The encourager within says, "Stay in the Word, always pray and meditate on the Word. Before speaking, seek guidance from God."

Don't copy the behavior and customs of this world, but let God transform you into a new person by changing the way you think (Rom. 12:2).

Stop allowing others to think for you. God gave each of us a mind, free will, and direct access to Him. He expects us to utilize it. Throughout this lifespan, there will be multiple decisions to make. You need not be self-righteous. A loving and gentle spirit will help communicate the standards in which you conduct yourself.

Don't condemn others. Recognize that Christ resides within you (once saved). He Himself is the new nature you have been blessed with. Christ is love, power, gentleness, self-control, etc. Therefore, we are to take on love, power, gentleness, self-control, etc., when interacting with others.

Christ is not only a loving God; He is a just God who loves order in our relationship.

Inwardly, we know when things are not quite right. The problem arises with the way some things are handled that causes division, lack of respect, lack of trust, and even lack of team spirit. The same problem when handled biblically, diplomatically, and with humility can create unity.

Initiating New Hope

It was the third month of Grace and Tatiana studying. Tatiana had grown and enjoyed studying with excitement! This time she was like a little girl rushing to share her good news.

On the way to the nursing home, Tatiana reminisced over the two previous lessons. *I can't wait to share with Grace the maturity I have received from our studies. Wait until she hears about how I had to drop some dead weight,* she thought, smiling. I know she will get a laugh from that. I never thought an old woman could bring such excitement, wisdom, and humor to a young person of my age.

As Tatiana signed in at the front desk, the nurse asked, "Are you here to see Grace?"

"Yes."

"Tatiana, can you go to room 137, and wait a moment."

"Sure," she said. "I guess she is getting ready to see me or is in with her doctor or something. I can wait."

The doctor came in to see Tatiana. "Hi, young lady. You must be Tatiana."

"Yes, sir. Are you Grace's doctor?"

"Yes. Tatiana, I have heard so many great things about you. Grace shared with everyone the laughter the two of you shared. I am sure you are aware of doctor-patient confidentially. That being said, Grace and her daughter signed a document giving me permission to share some information with you. He handed Tatiana a copy of the document.

Tatiana asked, "What do you mean shared? Where is Grace?"

The doctor responded, "I am sorry to inform you that Grace passed away Monday morning. Tatiana, words cannot express the smile and glow on Grace's face when she spoke of you. As her physician, I can assure you, your visits brought joy to a lonely lady. Yes, she had family, but they didn't come to the nursing home to see her, so she anxiously awaited your visits. During the days in between your visits, she was preparing something for you. She asked two weeks ago if I would give this box to you in the event something happened to her. I hope you will continue to come visit others here. You have so much to offer. Will you still consider ministering to others here?"

"Can I get back to you on that? I am not saying no, I just need a little time. I was looking forward to seeing Grace today. May I sit in this room for a little while?"

"Sure, I understand. If there is anything I can do, please contact me. Here is my number."

Tatiana became overwhelmed with tears. What was she going to do now? Grace was her motivator, teacher, and friend. Who would she talk to and study with now?

As she opened the box, there was a picture of her and Grace praying. She never knew one was taken. On the back of the picture was written:

> Prayer will sustain you, never stop. God is only a prayer away. Remember the Holy Spirit is the encourager who lives within you. Read your Word daily. Study and meditate on God's word, and look to God for direction.

There were some paperwork. Tatiana thought it was accidentally placed in the box until she read it. It was addressed to her.

> I Maggie Thumptome, being of sound mind, give power of attorney to Tatiana Wilsonsth. Listed are two of my bank accounts I am turning over to her and request that she be executor of my estate. My daughter and I have discussed and agreed to this transaction. My estate has little value because I did not spend, just saved my money because I lived in the nursing home. Tatiana may do as she feels with everything except my Bible. I am requesting that she keep it for studying. My total assets between the two bank accounts and material items here and there come to the amount of two million dollars. All funeral arrangements have

been taken care of and paid for. (That is what I was doing when I didn't see you).

I have placed the remainder two bank accounts and home in Florida to be given to my daughter who resides in Florida. It comes to three million dollars.

The next paper stated:

Tatiana, never forget the fire that is stirred up within you. You have a new hope. Like the dry bones, you must hear the word of the Lord in order to live. The Lord is the first and the last (Isa. 44:6b).

Regardless of your situation, remember Ezekiel 37:11–14 and remember three things.

1. Tap into God who is your true source of power.

2. When feeling hopeless or challenged, think about Jesus is your hope. He said, "I am the way, the truth, and the life."

3. When losing direction, tap into the best GPS guide in the world, the Holy Spirit. You are never alone. Jesus said he will not leave you alone.

You must import God's word into your heart before you can effectively export God's truth. It's time out for outward worship and empty inward praise. It's time out for focusing on manly accolades and titles based on what others say. It's time out for judging others based upon third-party opinions and what you think or feel about someone or event. It's time out for saying you are called and acting like you called yourself. Pick up that dusty Bible that is on your table for decoration and read it. Learn it (Rom. 12:2). Live it (Phil. 4:9), and loan it (Titus 2:7–8).

Set your affection on things above, not on things on the earth (Col. 3:2).

Tatiana, at this time, I know you can't hear me singing. But the song in my heart is.

> "It pays to serve Jesus/it pays every day/and it pays every step of the way/though the pathway to glory may sometimes be drear/you'll be happy each step of the way." (Song Title: It Pays to Serve Jesus; by Frank C. Huston. The New National Baptist Hymnal, page 402, copyright 1977).

This is my prayer.
Grace

As you are reading this book, what do you think should be Tatiana's next step?

Impossibility to Man, Possibility to God

What is impossible with men is possible with God. (Luke 18:27 NIV).

In this passage, Jesus is counseling to the rich young ruler. The ruler wants to know what he must do to inherit eternal life. He presents a resume of the commandments he has kept. Jesus asks him to sell all that he has and distribute to the poor. The ruler was not all that happy with this request.

Take a moment and write out your kept commandments. What was the real reason you kept them? What is the real reason you have not kept them? Is your reason man focused or God focused?

Commandment	Kept and Why	Not Kept and Why	God Focused or Man Focused

I have not been happy with some requests made of me. However, if it is best for kingdom building, I usually come through. Just like some of you reading this book. We have all experienced requests asked of us by God and/or others that did not make us happy, or we just did not understand why. There are times in one's life when you may have challenges and not understand. Some examples are the following:

1. Financially, not being able to do some things when it came to fellowshipping with the saints at events, conferences, luncheons, shopping, etc. You sacrificed and did it so people wouldn't talk about you. Unfortunately, people sometime assume everything is all right, and you just did not want to attend. Ever consider asking the person if they are okay? And not asking for details on their personal business. Ever consider just praying for the person just in case they are experiencing challenges?

2. Have you ever experienced this? How did you handle it, or did you handle it?

3. Why when a person is quiet, do some people assume something is wrong? Sometimes people become quiet because it might appear every time they give constructive suggestions or feedback, some people take it as being negative or complaining. If this has happened to you, were you referred to as being annoying? Wow, did you ever imagine giving

constructive suggestions would take on the form of annoying? Imagine how that would hurt with so many people doing and saying things that are not accurate all around you. Take a moment and think how you feel when being ignored, passed over, and decisions were made based on a third party's words or thoughts about you. When experiencing this, pray, wait for instructions from God, and remember there will be times when you need to just be quiet, listen, and move when God or if God gives you instructions to.

4. It pays to be quiet and depend on God. You see, at times, you may be the obstacle in preventing your own blessings. Being quiet is not a bad thing. Your words when not thought out, prayed over, and given in a diplomatic manner can mess you up. Believe it or not, your words can prophesy your own defeat. Therefore, God said to be careful of the words you speak.

Let's do an evaluation.

1. When some people make suggestions, why do people feel they are trying to take their position?

2. Why do people use other people's ideas and suggestions then act like it came from them?

3. Why do people ask others questions concerning you, which should be answered by you, only to receive answers from others and act upon their response without consulting with you? I am sure you know how to say yes, no, or maybe.

4. Why do some people appear to struggle so much when all they do is work, go to church, and go home?

If Jesus asks you to sell all that you have and distribute it to people who have wronged you, how would you feel? Would you do it? Would you do it unselfishly with a clear mind and a clean heart without a second thought?

God is asking you to stop looking at others and look to Him. Reevaluate your schedule. Where is your focus, and who is the majority of your time focused on? God knows your thoughts. He knows your weaknesses. Most of all, He knows your heart. For in His Word it states,

> Likewise the Spirit helps in our weakness. For we do not know what we should pray for, but the Spirit Himself makes intercession for us with groanings which cannot be uttered. (Romans 8:26 NKJV)

Once you stop and really listen to God, you will immediately start downsizing some things. Your schedule will no longer be more people focused than God focused. Stop looking for accolades, encouragement, value, or simple acknowledgement and appreciation from man. Wow, man does not define who you are. God defines you!

God has gifted you, and God will see you through when going through the challenges of life. God is your personal encourager, protector, provider and, yes, comforter! The Holy Spirit (the encourager within you) is your guide, your warning indicator and your comforter.

The Encourager in Luke 18:27 require a relationship with your heart. There is not one person on planet Earth who does not lack in something. The one thing you lack in may be the one thing God through the Holy Spirit instructs you to make an adjustment in. Some examples of things people may need an adjustment in are: (1) specific and *clear* communication, (2) *method* of communication and, (3) *physical* movements when communicating.

Clear communication involves simple, clear goals. When a person states or appears not to understand what you are saying, please be considerate of your response. Did you give accurate information? How many times had the same information been revised? How many people are distributing the information? This alone is not communicating clearly. I have been in situations where a person thought I was playing when I really did not understand. All this did was frustrate me. I would dismiss the person and conversations by saying, "You are right," or "I got it." Sometimes, the way a person would look at me when talking to me would do the same. This is because the conversation was communicated as if I was not to smart or maybe the person felt like they had said the same thing several times already, or the person assumed I did not know how. Clear communication involves not reacting off false information received from a third party or unclear directions.

Imagine if God was to say, in my Word, I have established a relationship between you through my Son. However, you ask too many questions, which I have already given you the answer to, so I am going to just keep you out the loop. How would you feel?

Have you ever told someone on a down low to just keep someone out the loop without a valid reason? Was it based on what you thought, or someone else said about the person? Or were you led by the Holy Spirit? It may be necessary in some cases. Analyze, if you did was it necessary? Was it handled with a biblical foundation? Or was it based emotionally?

The encourager within you here informs you to "hold fast the pattern of sound words…in faith and love" (2 Tim. 1:13 NKJV). In this passage, Paul is encouraging Timothy to stand strong and remember the sound doctrine he was taught. When Jesus ministered to others, He spoke clearly, precisely, and He moved on. When questions were asked of Him, He answered honestly, directly, and in a way the person receiving the answer would understand.

I had to learn the hard way that some people just do not know how to communicate. However, we are all capable of learning how to be more effective with communication when given the chance. One of the things that use to bother me was when people would ask others questions that should be directed to me. Do not assume anyone knows me better than I know what I am capable of. Only person who knows me better than myself is God! Do not assume all Christians who communicate to you communicate in a way that is pleasing in the eyes of God.

Lack of communication, unfortunately, can push people away. It can create lack of trust, lack of teamwork, lack of enthusiasm, and lack of participation. This can also be based upon an individual's level of spiritual maturity. The encourager within you here informs you, "Whatever you do, do it heartily, as to the Lord and not to men" (Col. 3:23 NKJV).

How we communicate and the method of communication is vital to everyone. No matter how awesome a person is at certain skills, talents, or gifts, it does not mean the method is correct. The less received and sometimes worst method of communication is through a third party. Third parties can cause confusion, division, and dissention. A person struggling within may simply pull away.

This is very important in ministry. The Bible tells us to do things decently and in order. If the method is out of order, if there is no structure, and things change on a daily basis based upon a selective mind-set at the time, based upon certain cliques or specific people, this causes a gap within the method of communicating with others. In other words, methods should always be based upon the bigger picture rather than the personal relationships and/ or attitudes of ownership. A person's title does not give you sole ownership over their every move.

Unless we find our identity primarily by our relationship with Christ, we will think we are grown and encounter unnecessary problems over time. Jesus described Himself as being in the Father, and the Father being in Him (John 14: 9–10). Jesus mirrored God exactly.

> Jesus said to him, "Have I been with you so long, and yet you have not known Me, Philip? He who has seen Me has seen the Father; so how can you say, 'Show us the Father'(John 14:9 NKJV)?
>
> "Do you not believe that I am in the Father, and the Father in Me? The words that I speak to you I do not speak on My own authority; but the Father who dwells in Me does the works."(John 14:10 NKJV)

When saved, the Holy Spirit takes up residence in us. As we study the Word, we learn more and more about God, all the while establishing a more intimate relationship with Him.

Of today's society people are so busy, doing what—I am not sure at time. It shows when it comes to planning our daily lives. I have heard many people ask and read many books asking, "What is my purpose here on earth?" Well, let's start with, "To honor and obey God by working diligently to follow the principles set forth in His Word."

When things are going well and when looking for direction or feeling down, this is the time to get on your knees and talk to the Lord. The direction you or I might choose may be so far from what God has chosen for us. The way of man is not in himself; it is not in man who walks to direct his own steps (Jeremiah 10:23 NKJV).

You need to find and study a source of spiritual direction and guidance from someone who really knows the answers (Isa.55:8–9).

We are not accidents, nor do we exist by chance. Before we take our first breath, God knows how long we'll live. "Your eyes saw my substance, being yet unformed. And in Your book they all were written, the days fashioned for me, when as yet there were none of them" (Ps. 139:16, NKJV).

God formed every complex detail of our bodies, minds, and spirits.. God placed humankind as living symbols of Himself on earth to represent His reign (kingdom).

But what do some people do instead? They focus on the details at hand—climbing the corporate ladder, accumulating material things, driving to every conceivable event (just because you can), participating in this or that committee, being the chair or president of more than five committees, having a name on the role as if there is no one else who can do it. Have you considered relinquishing one or more of your many titles to someone who is capable of accomplishing it as well? If not, why? Is your reason biblical, personal, emotional or self-righteous? Do you think the person is not qualified? How did you come to this conclusion? Was it biblically based or another?

We've lost sight of the big picture. Take a hard look at your to-do list. Is there anything on it that is going to develop your relationship with God? Is there something on it that might not be pleasing to Him? What can you cross off and exchange for something with real and lasting significance? I am not saying all the areas/committees do not have significance. I am saying where is your passion? Why do you feel you have to hold so many titles? Are you making quality time for home? Are you making quality time for God outside of the church and many meetings/events you are attending? If married, how much quality time are you making for your spouse outside of fellowshipping with church members; I mean, alone with your spouse?

Some people are mistaken about the purpose of life. Some pursue riches and material possessions—a bigger house, newer car, nicer clothes and furniture. Some pursue pleasure—entertainment, recreation, travel, etc. Life has no higher purpose than "Fun, fun, fun," "Be a party animal," "Eat, drink, and be merry, for tomorrow we die." Some pursue education. They seek to accumulate knowledge and worldly wisdom. What is your pursuit in life?

Man's finite mind can never imagine even with technology and the brilliant minds of scientist the power of God. For when I think about how God communicated creation in just six days. Let's for one moment stop and take a look around. Look at the stars, sun, moon, mountains, and sky, etc. God is beyond what you or I may imagine.

> For My thoughts are not your thoughts, neither are your ways My ways, saith the Lord. For as the heavens are higher than the earth, so are My ways higher than your ways, And My thoughts than your thoughts. (Is. 55:8–9 KJV)

This same God (Encourager) resides within you after you give your life to Him. The Scripture says that God's very nature is love. God never functions contrary to his own nature. Never will God express His Will toward you except through an expression of perfect love. God's kind of love always seeks the very best for a person. Therefore, He can never give you second best. His will always give His best, His directions are always right and He is interested in an intimate relationship with you.

We develop an intimate relationship by first communicating with God. Communication begins with prayer.

The Bible gives the real purpose of life. In Ecclesiastes 2:1–11 and 12:13–14, Solomon experienced the pinnacle of enjoyment in every aspect of life—wealth, pleasure, and wisdom. Did it satisfy Solomon? It was all "vanity and vexation of spirit" (2:11). In Matthew 6:19–24, 33, the real goal of life is to work in God's kingdom and be right before Him. God created man for a purpose. Life is meaningless unless we fulfill that purpose.

We are to learn to walk in a mature spiritual way. This does not mean you can not have fun. As Christians begin to walk, they also begin to fellowship with others. Do not be deceived; "Evil company corrupts good habits" (1 Cor. 15:33).

Your choice of friends has greater significance than simply the pleasures of the day. When you choose your friends based upon positive values, you are living out a principle that is repeated throughout the Bible: you need to choose your friends and companions carefully, since your relationships will, in large part, determine whether you stay the course of faith.

> Many people will walk in and out of your life, but only true friends will leave footprints in your heart. (Eleanor Roosevelt)
>
> Friendship is an honest mirror, but it must be allowed to reflect or its power is lost. (Mary Hunt)
>
> The righteous should choose his friends carefully, for the way of the wicked leads them astray. (Prov. 12:26)
>
> Not everyone who says to Me, "Lord, Lord," shall enter the kingdom of heaven, but he who does the will of My Father in heaven. (Matt. 7:21)

Be careful what we speak and how we act, for people imitate their parents, peers, leaders, and popular celebrities to name a few. As iron sharpens iron, so people can improve each other (Prov. 27:17). Good role models can help. Iron sharpens iron by showing as role models what is possible. Example: how the "son of thunder" can become the "apostle of love" (Mark 3:17; Luke 9:54; 1 John 4:7–8). Another example, how "uneducated and untrained men" can boldly proclaim the gospel of Christ (Acts 4:13).

If you seek to grow spiritually, take advantage of positive role models. Let them show you what is possible! Let them teach you how to obtain the goals you are striving for! Let them encourage you to persevere, knowing that others have traveled the same path before you!

Prayer

An essential part of starting the day is through prayer. You pray to the Father, in the name of the Son, in the Spirit. Give reference to God first, pray for others second, pray God's will be done third, and then make your request known unto God.

Pray for Scriptures

Take consideration of the assignment of outreach and reconciliation. As Christians, we are to focus on the people we are trying to reach. Look at the occasions, circumstances, and needs that are in the public mind, for example, the "variety of school shootings." This was only a few of the devastations that have occurred in this day and age. The city, state, and nation became one in prayer when these tragedies happened. Are we as a nation continuing to pray for the families affected personally from these shootings? We must remain in prayer at all times. We are to pray in good and bad times.

Prayer is communicating with God. When witnessing or encouraging others, ask God for guidance on which scriptures to share. To do this, you must study the Bible daily, and the Holy Spirit will bring remembrance the right scripture at the right time to you.

As stated earlier, keep a notebook to write down ideas from sermons, insights, books, illustrations, etc. Write your thoughts immediately because you may forget them later.

Pray to maintain your focus. Your expressions should be
short, clear, vivid sentences.

As our communication with God increase daily through prayer, our hearts change. The bitter, insecure, timid person becomes a positive, strong, bold person for Christ. David said in Psalm 51:10 (kjv), "Create in me a clean heart." He had a desire to change. Change starts within the heart. A person who is not in church may ask, "How can I receive a clean heart? What does David mean create in me a clean heart?"

So let's break down the word *clean*. In the *Strong's Concordance* the word *clean* is entry number 02889 and is defined as "(1) clean; ceremonial of animals, (2) pure; physically and, (3) pure, clean (morally, ethically)."

David realized the only way his heart could truly be fixed and reflect God was to have a surgical procedure that only God could be the doctor.

God, the author and finisher of this universe, sees our heart. Humility, patience, and faith comes from the heart. We were created for service, and everything we do should glorify God. Our actions and speech can fool the most educated person, for they see outward, but God sees the inward and outward of our thoughts and actions.

A Heart That Glorifies God

And ye shall seek Me, and find Me, when ye shall search for Me with your whole heart.

—Jeremiah 29:13

God knows our thoughts. He knows our weaknesses. Most of all, He knows our heart. In His Word, he states,

In the same way the Spirit helps us in our weakness. We do not know what we ought to pray for, but the Spirit Himself intercedes for us with groans that words cannot express. And He who searches our hearts knows the mind of the Spirit. (Rom. 8:26)

As we mature spiritually in Christ, we learn to stand firm and secure in God's word and love. Standing is learning to depend totally on God. "I can do all things through Christ who strengthens me" (Phil. 4:13). This means God will never give an assignment and leave you unequipped to accomplish the task. A friend of mine e-mailed the following statement to me one day, "The will of God will never take you where the grace of God will not protect you."

When God sent His Son Jesus, born of a virgin, let him walk in the flesh on this earth as a man, Jesus knew He was born to die. Yet He went about His Father's business, teaching, preaching, healing, and saving souls. He took on the sins of the world that we may have a chance at eternal life.

We acknowledge that sin is still a powerful force in today's society, but it cannot control you unless you allow it to do so. When asking for help from God, trust in the Lord and the guidance of the Holy Spirit. The Bible says,

> Blessed is the man who trusts in the Lord, And whose hope is the Lord. For he shall be like a tree planted by the waters, Which spreads out its roots by the river, And will not fear when heat comes; But its leaf will be green, And will not be anxious in the year of drought, Nor will cease from yielding fruit.

You cannot effectively reference scriptures or speak on God if you do not know and have a personal relationship with God. Part of having a personal relationship with God is reading your Bible as you develop a more intimate relationship with God. Throughout this book, cross references are applied to the Bible. Let's take a moment to briefly explain what the Bible is.

What Is the Holy Bible?

The Bible is our spiritual heritage. This book is comprised of sixty-six smaller books written over approximately 1,600 years by authors inspired by God. The Bible gives inspiration to billions of people worldwide because it is God's word.

Christian Faith

God's Word informs us that we must believe in His Son, Jesus Christ, for the Christian faith is founded on Jesus Christ and His resurrection. Since this is the foundation of the Christian faith, then the historical veracity of Jesus' life, death, and resurrection are essential to Christianity. Christian faith is not based upon "faith and no works," it's not about turning off the brain and merely relying on the heart or squashing reason in favor of emotion. It is about seeking and knowing Jesus Christ in an intimate way. It is about loving him with all your heart, mind, soul, and strength.

Who Is Jesus?

1. *The way*—we are not asked to follow men or religion but to follow Jesus.

2. *The truth*—God's truth is in the Word of God, the Holy Bible.

3. *The life*—there is no life without knowing Him.

As stated earlier, The Old Testament Prophesied about Jesus.

1. God will declare the Messiah (Jesus) to be His Son. (Ps. 2:7)

2. All things would be placed under the Messiah's feet. (Ps. 8:6)

3. His throne will be forever. (Ps. 45:6)

4. He will ascend to God's right hand. (Ps. 68:18)

5. He will pray for His enemies. (Ps. 109:4)

Jesus Endured Ridicule to Redeem Man.

1. God will forsake Him in His hour of need. (Ps. 22:1)

2. He will be mocked and insulted. (Ps. 22:7–8)

3. His hands and feet will be pierced. (Ps. 22:16)

4. He will be accused by ruthless witnesses. (Ps. 35:11)

5. He will be hated without any reason. (Ps. 35:19)

6. He will be betrayed by a friend. (Ps. 41:9)

The New Testament Fulfilled Prophecy from the Old Testament.

1. This is My beloved Son, in whom I am well pleased. (Matt. 3:17)

2. You have put all things in subjection under His feet. (Heb. 2:8)

3. But to the Son He says, "Your throne, O God, is forever and ever; A scepter of righteousness is the scepter of Your kingdom." (Heb. 1:8)

4. So then, after the Lord had spoken to them, He was received up into the heaven, and sat down at the right hand of God. (Mark 16:19)

5. Then Jesus said, "Father forgive them, for they do not know what they do." (Luke 23:34)

6. And about the ninth hour Jesus cried out with a loud voice saying, "Eli, Eli, lama sabachthani?" That is, My God, My God, why have You forsaken Me?" (Matt. 27:46)

7. And the people stood looking on. But even the rulers with them sneered, saying, "He saved others; let Him save Himself if He is the Christ, the chosen of God." (Luke 23:35)

8. The other disciples therefore said to him, "We have seen the Lord." So he said to them, "Unless I see in His hands the print of the nails, and put my finger into the print of the nails, and put my hand into His side, I will not believe. Then He said to Thomas, "Reach your finger here, and look at My hands; and reach your hand here, and put it into My side. Do not be unbelieving, but believing. (John 20:25, 27)

9. Then some rose up and bore false witness against Him. (Mark 14:57)

10. But this happened that the word might be fulfilled which is written in their law, They hated Me without a cause. (John 15:25)

11. And while He was still speaking, behold, a multitude; and he who was called Judas, one of the twelve, went before them and drew near to Jesus to kiss Him. (Luke 22:47)

> A child of God needs to know God for himself or herself. Know God's word, live it, and it must be heartfelt. Once we accept the Lord in our life, His spirit will abide in us. For when Jesus died, He said, "I would send unto you a comforter.(John 15:26)"

> But if the Spirit of him that raised up Jesus from the dead dwell in you, he that rose up Christ from the dead shall also quicken your mortal bodies by his Spirit that dwelleth in you. (Rom. 8:11 NKJV)

> I charge you not to give up hope or become discouraged and lay in this spirit of defeat or despair. God has a plan for your life before you even think about what you want to do with your life.

> Ye have not chosen me, but I have chosen you, and ordained you, that ye should go and bring forth fruit, and that your fruit should remain: that whatsoever ye shall ask of the Father in My name, He may give it you. (John 15:16, KJV)

Jesus voluntarily chose to lay down His life for us. No man took His life. In return, He asks us to *believe* (John 3:16, John 20:31) we are saved through faith (Rom. 1:17). Once we are saved, we are sealed with the Holy Spirit (Eph.1:13).

When there is a deep passion within you to know God, your praise and worship is unique, humble, loving, and not arrogant or boastful.

When you accept Christ, the process of spiritual growth begins. The new nature, which is that of a newborn baby, has to be nurtured with God's word for growth and development. The word of God is necessary food for the soul, which does not leave you the same but improves you, causing you to realize your spiritual position in the world, the duty of loving, diplomatic patience, Christlike submission, and the necessity of purging out those things from life which are contrary to Christ.

Spiritual growth is detailed in 2 Peter 1:3–8.

> His divine power has given us everything we need for life and godliness through our knowledge of Him who called us by His own glory and goodness. Through these He has given us His very great and precious promises, so that through them you may participate in the divine nature and escape the corruption in the world caused by evil desires. For this very reason, make every effort to add to your faith goodness; and to goodness, knowledge; and to knowledge, self-control; and to self-control, perseverance; and to perseverance, godliness; and to godliness, brotherly kindness; and to brotherly kindness, love. If you possess these qualities in increasing measure, they will keep you from being ineffective and unproductive in your knowledge of our Lord Jesus Christ (2 Peter 1:-9 NIV).

Therefore, spiritual growth includes: (1) increasing in your knowledge and understanding of God's Word; (2) decreasing in your frequency and severity of sin; (3) increasing in your practice of Christlike qualities; and (4) increasing in your faith and trust in God; and (5) decreasing self that God may increase. Perhaps, the best summary of spiritual growth is becoming more like Jesus Christ.

Many problems result when members fail to grow. Some go back to the world; others cause strife because of lack of knowledge or become stumbling blocks because of irregular attendance, worldliness, or indifference.

The maturity level grows and we become steadfast, constantly in communication with God through prayer, meditation, and daily devotionals. Our passion within yearns to learn more and more. In my words, you take on the symbolic meaning of a sponge; you're eager to learn every day, realizing our purpose is to give God the glory and give your best in everything you do.

Steps toward living according to God's Word:

1. *Pray* daily

2. *Study* God's Word daily

3. Establish a *daily* devotional life

4. *Meditate* on God's Word daily

5. Be a *living* witness daily

6. Be *obedient* to God's Word daily

Put on God's armor (Eph. 6:13–18).

1. *Belt of Truth:* truth and honesty bind Christians together.

2. *Breastplate of Righteousness:* purity as a way of life daily.

3. *Gospel of Peace*: s trong, united relationships

4. *Shield of Faith:* the Christians strength comes from God.

5. *Helmet of Salvation:* assurance of protection

6. *Sword of the Spirit:* the Bible

Unfortunately, we live in a world were no matter how hard you try, some people judge you based upon your appearance, your material possessions, your education, your leadership position within the church or lack of, and your attendance to various events within the church.

What Does My Appearance Say About My Growth

We are all leaders in some capacity. Some people are gifted and assigned positions to oversee others. We should have a humble heart that reaches out and prays for all persons in leadership positions every day. Ask God to watch over persons in leadership positions (i.e. president, pastor, supervisors etc.) to give them knowledge, wisdom, patience, and understanding, for everyone is not going to receive what he or she is saying.

God's Word is very precise with giving instruction for every aspect of a person's life. When sharing God's Word, we are not to rearrange it.

> Ye shall not add unto the word which I command you, neither shall ye diminish aught from it, that ye may keep the commandments of the Lord your God which I command you. (Deut. 4:2 KJV)

Share God's Word as given by the Holy Spirt. Be a positive impact in your home, church and community.

Step on some toes! Turn some heads! For God's' word is a double-edged sword. It should touch every part of our life and penetrate our heart. For the word of God is quick, powerful, sharper, and piercing even to the dividing asunder of soul and spirit and of the joints and marrow and is a discerner of the thoughts and intents of the heart (Heb. 4:12).

When a preacher/pastor is giving a sermon and everything said is coming directly from Gods word, with scripture to back it up, why complain and change what was said? Instead, read the scriptures given, then pray, and if something comes upon you and your situation, ask God to give you direction and understanding.

Man can see the external and be fooled. However, God dwells within, changes occur, and it shows on the outside. For the real person is within your heart.

> But the Lord said unto Samuel, Look not on his countenance, or on the height of his stature; because I have refused him, for the Lord seeth not as man seeth; for man looketh on the outward appearance, but the Lord looketh on the heart. (1 Sam. 16:7 KJV)

One example of outer appearance shows with the clothes we wear. Please, respect Gods place of worship. Bring respectful etiquette back into the church. If someone doesn't have the proper clothing, this shouldn't prevent them from coming to church. Still come to church. Persons in church shouldn't turn around and stare or look at the person in a demeaning manner. Judge not according to the appearance, but judge righteous judgment (John 7:24).

For people who have been blessed with some nonrevealing, tight-fitting clothing and choose to wear tight-fitted, revealing clothing to church, ask yourself, are you truly representing God's kingdom?

Ladies (married and single), men in church are human. How do we expect them to focus when we so eloquently stroll by with an outfit so tight or low cut or too short? What do you expect them to do besides get distracted? Men (married and single), women in church are human too. How do you expect them to focus when you so muscularly approach a female with non-biblical intentions?

Do you care about how you dress? What is your heart saying with the outfit you have on today?

1. Your body is the temple (1 Cor. 6:19–20).

2. Beauty is within (1 Tim. 2:9–10).

In spite of this, we are to still love and pray for each other. Take time to learn more about building relationships, attend seminars, and conferences. With the knowledge received you can assist with some positive ideas.

Think About It

1. What does the clothing we wear today say about our character?

2. What do the clothes our children wear say about their character?

3. What does society say about the clothing we wear?

4. What does the Bible say about the clothing we wear?

The response of some people within the congregation unfortunately can affect the next step a person takes toward their spiritual growth. One may never know who is wearing a mask. Many people wear their heart on their sleeve and just as many have a customized mask they wear daily.

A mask is something used to cover up something else. It can be visible or invisible. It can be small or something big.

The mask most people deal with today is internal and invisible, customized to operate within their daily schedule. They were placed as a form of protection. Or maybe you can say the problem/s were placed behind a closed door rather than dealt with, waiting for an opportunity to surface once again. These chances usually occur when you seem to be headed down the right road.

Today, it is so natural to wear an invisible mask as part of our wardrobe. After all, the purpose of a mask is to cover up issues. However, when the mask is removed, you're considered to have issues.

There is no mask that God can't see through. For whatever reason you felt you needed a mask, stop a moment, talk to God about the mask you are now wearing, and wait for a response. Sometimes, people wear mask to achieve the appearance of perfection.

News flash: you are not perfect, and this world is not perfect!

There are people who are going to annoy you, talk about you, and lie about you on purpose or conveniently say it was by accident. There will be times when you will be determined to move forward, be in a good mood, have a good day, look good etc. Then from nowhere, someone or something inadvertently irritates you for whatever the reason may be. Then what happens? We begin to think negative thoughts or decide this is not for us, or we don't have to take this, and all of a sudden, we've customize a mask to fit into our daily routine.

What you should have done was pray over the situation before taking the step. I didn't say stop and pray for two hours. You can say, "Lord, help me," "Lord, give me the words to say," or just, "Lord, what do you want me to do."

Don't allow someone to steal your joy, where you have no peace. The word of God says, "Peace I leave with you, My peace I give unto you, not as the world give it, I give it. Let not your heart be troubled neither let it be afraid" (John 14:27 NKJV)

We were "saved to serve," not "saved to sit." The day you gave your life to the Lord, somebody got bad, jealous, and maybe even a little envious of you. Don't let that light go out by thinking now that you are saved, you are better than people. Or even worst by thinking now that you are saved, all you have to do is go to church on Sundays, every other Wednesday, a couple of programs, and this will give you a ticket to heaven. I don't think so!

There is written nowhere that God promised you a carefree life. A person who never encounters problems or run into distractions and obstacles should stop and do a self-analysis. Could it be that you are part of the problem or part of a group associated with the problem.

Learn that with God's help and the help of the Holy Spirit, which dwells in us, we can overcome things that are contrary to God's word. In the book of Matthew Chapter 28 verses nineteen through 20, we have been commissioned to go out into the world and share the good news about God. We have an assignment as servants to help others. Sometimes, it may seem extremely difficult to spread the gospel to nonreceptive ears. Just remember the gospel is a message from God in heaven to a sinful world.

Read these scriptures and think.

1. 2 Samuel 22:2–4 lift up your eyes to the hills, know where your help comes from.

2. Genesis 15:6; trust God without any reservations.

3. James 5:10–11; be patient and faithful in all circumstances.

In order to achieve progress, you have to go through a process. It is not going to happen overnight. Ask for God's help. When God places that dream or vision in our mind, he supplies us with the tools to see it through. God did not create a dream He could not fulfill.

Everyone has endured a storm in his or her life. Some self-created and some are test of our faith. Others may be from people who are just mean and maybe jealous of you or your gifts.

Storms Are Not Gender Selective

The common factor here is male or female, either has or will experience the storms of life. During these storms, people can become vulnerable because everyone is not on the same level of faith. Therefore, people endure storms differently. We state we have the victory. However, when problems arise, our actions show defeat. Has this ever happened to you? If so, how did you handle it?

We state how God is with us before, during, and after the storm, yet when it is our turn to endure a storm, we fall apart like grains of sand. Some never recover from a personal storm. Some become living testimonies. This is due in retrospect to how your storm is handled. Is self the source of your direction, or is it God?

When dealing with the problem(s), some people laugh at you, talk about you, lie on you, say you're crazy, or just don't understand you. Others stand by you, help you, and pray for and with you. Sound familiar? Yes, "For God so loved the world that He gave His only begotten Son" (John 3:16a NKJV). Jesus came to heal, encourage, save, and correct what man so diligently messed up. In return, some people laughed at him, talked about him, lied on him, said He was crazy, or just didn't understand him. Others stood by him, showed love toward him, and prayed with him.

Jesus, being the Son of God, still was obedient to His Father and endured the cross at Calvary (God's will and plan). So what makes you think you can go through life happy go lucky with no storms as you carry your cross or think no cross for you to bare? The problem is not the storm we are in but how we come through the storm/s.

The Bible informs us that we are to make our bodies a living (emphasis on *living*) sacrifice. How can you be a living testimony if you never endure your storm? How can you endure the storm, unless you have a solid foundation to stand on? Your foundation is found in the Bible. Your personal relationship is engraved on your heart. When you know without a doubt who you are and who you are, stand! God said you are either for me or against me. You are out of order if you stand for God on Sunday and worldly on Monday through Saturday. If this is the case, your problem/s can become unstable.

Storms Affect Young and Old

As parents, mentors, leaders etc. make time to listen to today's children and youth. Do not tune them out. Listen attentively from the heart. Take time out to say, "Thank you for sharing your thoughts, goals, and dreams with me." The mind of a child is very active. If we take the time out to place our love for a child in action, they will always amaze you with their intellect and eagerness to succeed.

The mind of a child is inquisitive when it involves knowledge, understanding, and acceptance. Their heart is sincere and easily hurt when at the end of an answer is a no responsive or inattentive reply. That is why it is so important how we speak, treat others, and function around our children and youth.

Yes, I received a solid foundation, attended church every Sunday. I attended so much until in my mind, I couldn't wait to turn eighteen. You know move out and make my own decisions, etc. The world was looking pretty good in my eyes when I graduated from high school. I wanted to take a break from church and experience what was out there. The outcome was creating an invisible mask, and going through life, battling little by little a storm at a time, I learned that I had established a relationship with the church. I hadn't established a heartfelt, personal relationship with God because I wasn't truly worshiping Him (true worship is a mind totally focused on God.)

I was going because my parents said go, and it was the thing to do. My parents were establishing a firm foundation that would help me through the storms of my life. Train up a child in the way he should go, and when he is old, he will not depart from it (Proverbs 22:6).

One time in my life, I thought if I make it fine as long as I wasn't hurting anyone or disrespecting anyone. However, my focus was on me, myself, and I; not God.

It wasn't until then as I identify my storm that I truly realize the power of my thoughts, words, and actions. My first thought was, *Lord why me*? It changed quickly to *why not me*?

You are never too young or too old to learn. Unfortunately, it took me a while to learn what I was doing. I was aware of it, just didn't follow it out to the end. Meaning, give it to the Lord and leave it there.

That's why it is important as parents to show an interest in your child's education, dreams, and people they associate with. Children and youth are exposed daily to unknown influences and/or challenges.

Children and youth need to know who they are and whom they are in (the Lord), as well as adults. They need to know how to function in a world that has no feelings for them.

Ask yourself the following questions:

1. Did I make study time in God's Word with my child today?

2. How much quality time did I give to my child today?

3. What lifestyle am I presenting before my child?

4. When approached with questions, how do I respond?

5. When they make a mistake, do I identify the problem first?

6. Do I resolve the problem in a positive manner?

According to your answers, may your child be wearing an invisible mask today?

Whether, you are a parent, guardian, and grandparent, etc., who is caring for a child, please read this section carefully.

Based upon technology and acceptance of friends and society, our children are growing up faster. This means they are at a higher risk when it comes to abuse. Abuse meaning, trying to fit in when they know within themselves it's wrong.

Some examples that can lead to this are the following:

1. Boyfriends/girlfriends who hit in the so-called name of love

2. Verbal criticism (because of their clothes, hair, shoes, intelligence, etc.)

3. Parents who allow them to dress and do anything until the parents are around someone they want to impress

4. Being around peers who use profanity and drink or smoke a lot.

God Is by Your Side;
Are You by God's Side?

God is invisible, and we can know only what we see. The Bible says, "Eye hath not seen, nor ear heard, neither have entered into the heart of man, the things which God hath prepared for them that love Him. God hath revealed them unto us by His Spirit" (1 Corinthians 2:9–10 KJV).

Jesus already informed us in His Word that trials and tribulations are a part of life. We have to persevere with the same determination in God's word that we do in our everyday routine of life. Continue to read, study, and live for Christ.

We are taught to endure patiently (1 Pet. 2:20). We must learn to have stability, continue in our commitments, walk in love, and help each other. Realize we cannot do anything without the Lord. When Jesus gives you that vision or goal, he will not leave you alone to accomplish it. You are equipped, you're not alone, and he'll send you help to complete your assignment.

When storms approach, they tend to open doors you thought were closed. Some of these newly opened doors feel like the worst storm of your life. You don't understand the whys, so you suppress or become depressed. This is due to the fact that you are not speaking to God about your storm. You are trying to balance it out yourself, or those so-called friends are telling you what they would do if it were their storm. Those same so-called friends are analyzing your problem in a negative manner (remember Job and his so-called friends).

This is when you need to realize who is your source (God), and you can't do it along. Thoughts run through your mind: What did I do? Did I cause this to happen to me? Why me? Are people looking at me? I am too strong for this to happen to me?

With some of my storms, I tried writing what I felt on paper. Talking it out never seemed to help me because I struggled trying to get my point across. Plus some of the people I spoke to didn't have my best interest at heart. Instead, I developed what I call my own personal brick wall. I became very quiet and watched everyone and everything around me, listening attentively.

I thought I healed from some storms. However, all I did was suppress them. This is a learning process for me. As I sit here typing, I am looking into a mirror of my life. It's ironic how later in life you see the mistakes that can cause or have caused a storm in your life.

When going through your storm

1. identify you can't solve this problem yourself.
2. Admit when or if you have made a mistake.
3. Ask for help if needed, not from any and everybody.
4. If the problem involves several people, ask for suggestions, and encourage participation from others.
5. Listen to people. Don't be so quick to cut them off
6. Don't mistreat anyone or assume that you know everything or are all of that.

"For the Lord giveth wisdom: out of His mouth cometh knowledge and understanding" (Proverbs 2:6 KJV). The only person, who truly knows what you are feeling in a storm and how to pull you through is the Lord. There are different types of storms that people deal with.

Emotional Storms

These are storms of the heart. The heart is considered to be the center of emotions, the innermost chamber of your thoughts and feelings.

Take a moment and think about how the body protects the heart. It is small, delicate, yet its function is to circulate blood throughout the body. What would happen if it just stopped? What would happen if it were physically damaged?

When dealing with sorrow or grief, you are determined not to get hurt like that again. Through all the protectiveness that you supply for yourself, it happens again. Now you become more protective and maybe frustrated. The devil tells you to handle it your way. You decide to either deal with it the wrong way or create a mask outwardly. What you should do is give it to the Lord. He is your heart fixer.

In some cases, the most precise yet hardened statement a person can make to you at this time is, "Things happen. "Move On." Use words of encouragement. Use a pleasant tone. Especially over the phone, a person can sense when you are not really listening. Be careful of your body language while listening attentively.

Emotional storms can affect your communication style. Some people feel, "Why should I? No one understand what I'm going through. No one wants to hear my sad story. No one can mend my heart. Some people don't listen. All they say is be quiet, and do what I say. You are too young to know anything about that. Go play, or do your homework."

If this is how you feel, please stop! You are not alone. Remove your mask, and allow the Lord to comfort and guide you.

Blessed be God, even the Father of our Lord Jesus Christ, the Father of compassion (mercy) and the God of all comfort, who comforts us in all our troubles so that we can comfort those in any trouble with the comfort we ourselves have received from God (2 Cor. 1:3–4).

Call on Jesus. He is someone who understands, has a listening ear, can mend your heart, will not say be quiet or you're too young.

Materialistic Storms

> Lay not up for yourselves treasures upon earth, where moth and rust doth corrupt, and where thieves break through and steal: But lay up for yourselves treasures in heaven, where neither moth nor rust doth corrupt, and where thieves do not break through nor steal: For where your treasure is, there will your heart be also. (Matthew 6:19–21 KJV)

When focusing only on material things, you create mini storms throughout your life. When I say mini storms, I am speaking on unnecessary worry over someone stealing it and problems created not being able to maintain it financially.

Focusing on material things can easily turn to greed. This can cause someone to almost lose their mind if a storm arises that removes their worldly possessions from them.

Our focus should be on the Lord and eternity. God knows our needs and desires.

We serve a mighty God who is owner of everything. When God supplies your needs, you want for nothing. He gives you what you can handle. The more you invest your time, talents, finances, etc., you'll be very well taken care of.

Spiritual Storms

The Lord informs us, you are either for Him or against Him. Spiritual storms may arise for growth. They may also arise due to disobedience. As long as we live, the enemy is going to go above and beyond to destroy you and your relationship with God.

Don't underestimate the tricks of the enemy.

1. Confusion of the mind

2. Illness of the body

3. Emptiness of the soul

4. Immoral practices

We are given the ability to choose whose side we are on. We are held accountable for the choices we make and the actions we take.

The Lord has given us the tools we need to fight this fight, along with free will. God is on your side, and that is the winning side. Don't allow the enemy to entice you with outward appearances of things and/or people. In other words, we must resist the devil.

Behold, I send you forth as sheep in the midst of wolves.

> Be ye therefore wise as serpents, and harmless as doves. But beware of men: they will deliver you up to the councils, and they will scourge you in their synagogues. (Matthew 10:16–17)

When dealing with spiritual storms, Paul informs us to endure hardness as a good soldier of Jesus Christ. Know with an unshakable foundation who you are and whose you are. Your colonel is the Lord. When fighting for righteousness, stand firm on God's word. This is your ammunition. Your uniform is as follows:

1. truth (knowledge of God's Word wrapped around you);
2. breastplate of righteous (character);
3. feet shod with the preparation of the gospel of peace (ready to witness);
4. shield of faith (God said it, and I believe it);
5. helmet of salvation (assurance);
6. sword of the spirit (the word of God).

Don't even think you can win on your own without the Lord. We can't even wake up on our own. God created all things. I have heard so many times the phrase, "I'm only human." This is true that we have limitations. It also means we will experience some physical storms.

Physical Storms

What? Know ye not that your body is the temple of the Holy Ghost which is in you, which ye have of God, and ye are not your own? For ye are bought with a price: therefore glorify God in your body, and in your spirit, which are God's. (1 Cor. 6:19–20 KJV)

As mentioned previously, Don't underestimate the tricks of the enemy.

1. Confusion of the mind
2. Illness of the body
3. Emptiness of the soul
4. Immoral practices

Pray and ask God when any storm arises in your life. Your faith, commitment, and continuance to learn, live, and share God's word will always pull you through.

When we are faced with trouble, God is our refuge. Think about where He's brought you from to where you are now. Think about God's goodness.

R	Righteousness
E	Eternity
M	Mercy
E	Empathy
M	Miracles
B	Blessings
E	Example
R	Redemption

Remember, you will be faced constantly with choices. You need not act self-righteous. A loving and gentle spirit will help you communicate that you have definite standards for your own conduct, although you do not condemn others. People will respect you for that spirit. Don't give up. Perseverance and persistence equals the prize! We must know our purpose because times will be difficult, and Satan will attack. The enemy is on his job 48/7, trying to destroy the saints. Each trial gets easier as you get stronger in the Lord.

Today, we have a widespread of material to read—study guides, maps, etc. We attend seminary schools, workshops, seminars, revivals, retreats, etc. There are so many speakers and people on TV and the radio. Knowledge can be found through all these various resources.

However, to apply all the knowledge we receive righteously, we must have a servant's heart. We must know who we are and whose we are, for God's kingdom is built on love. How can we say we are helping to build the kingdom when our heart is so far from God's ways?

God never promised us an easy carefree life. There will be trials and tribulations. If you are reading this book and have never had problems or run into obstacles, stop a moment. Now do a self-analysis. Are you part of or the cause of problem? Don't copy the behavior and customs of this world, but let God transform you into a new person by changing the way you think (Rom. 12:2).

- Believe in your heart that God can help.
- Trust in heart that God will help.
- Follow in your heart God's directions when given.

As you spend more and more time with the Lord, you feel His presence and love more and more. To know Him is to know love, patience, and kindness. God will give you strength to make it through. He's there when you need someone to give your burdens to, to see you through the unexplainable, and to help you reach the unattainable. He's just a whisper away. Don't give up! Stand strong in the Lord. You may not have the answer every time. Don't worry about that because no one has the answer every time. Continue to study and apply God's Word in your life knowing that

1. Psalm 33:6-7, "By the Word of the Lord all things were created."

2. John 14:6, "Jesus is the way, the truth, and the life"

3. John 14:26, "He'll send me a Comforter, to teach me, and bring remembrance to me."

4. Acts 16:31, "When you believe on the Lord, thy and thy house shall be saved."

There are no storms too large or too hard for God to calm. There is no mask that God can't see through. There is no problem that God can't solve. If you want peace in the midst of your storm, if you are tired of wearing that invisible customized mask, I would like to recommend for you to give Jesus a try.

Jesus is waiting for you to accept Him in your life today, believe within your heart that he'll make a way, confess your sins, and ask for forgiveness that you may receive salvation. Just open your heart, and ask the Lord to come in right now.

If you are not sure who I am talking about, let me give you a short refresher course. Let's take a journey to learn about a man whose heart is so full of love that He died for many. This man was rejected and mistreated, yet his love is undying. Even though he was mistreated, neither he nor his father took vengeance. They still loved us enough to offer everyone a chance to get it right. This man has many names:

Son of Man: "Even as the Son of man came not to be ministered unto, but to minister, and to give his life a ransom for many." (Matt. 20:28 kjv)

Heir of all things:

Jesus: There's something about the name "Jesus."

> Jesus the author and finisher of our faith; who for the joy that was set before him endureth the cross, despising the shame, and is set down at the right hand of the throne of God. (Heb. 12:2)

Exhibits

Do you know the real encourager?

Date Received: June 2015

Assembly Number: 70–71 members

Encourager's Name: God the Father, God the Son, and God the Holy Spirit

Below is the summary of activities telling you about the Son who volunteered His life for man. This case synopsis was presented in a court class years ago by the author of "An Encourager is Within You."

1 | Trinity Law Firm
2 | 3-N-1 Worldwide Lane
  | Straight Gate, Entrance 11137
3 | Phone: Universal Line
  | heavenlybound@eternity.com
4

5

6

7 | **SUPERIOR COURT OF KNOW HIM**
  | **COUNTY OF YOURSELF**
8

9

10

11
   | JESUS CHRIST, | Case No.: DRH2015
12
13 | Plaintiff,
   | | AN ENCOURAGEMENT IS WITHIN YOU
14 | vs.
15 | HUMANITY,
16 | Defendant

17

18

19 | The Trinity Law Firm, is a universal firm licensed by the Creator, God the Father,
20 | responsible for the universal creation of all things and salvation of sinners, hereby consents and
21 | joins in the adoption petition filed by the above-named Petitioner. Because of Jesus death on
22 | Calvary a comforter whose name is the Holy Spirt shall indwell in all persons once they receive
23 | Jesus Christ in their life.
24

25

26

27 | Dated this day of publication for the book of "An Encourager is Within You"

28

29

30

31 | *Deborah R. Hamm*
32 | Author Name

AN ENCOURAGEMENT IS WITHIN YOU - 1

CASE SUMMARY

Below is a summary of activities informing us about a Son who voluntarily gave His life as a ransom for mankind. This case synopsis was presented years ago in a class taught by the author of "An Encourager is Within You."

PERSON OR AGENCY ABOUT WHICH COMPLAINT IS MADE

Name: Jesus Christ

Address: Born in the West Bank (Galilean) Region (Bethlehem)

Bloodline: Descendent of David

NATURE OF COMPLAINT

Events are described in the order they occurred as clearly as clearly and concisely as possible. Documentation was received through research of the Sanhedrin Assembly A.K.A. Sanhedrin Council. Please note: the Sanhedrin Assembly has no jurisdiction over Death Penalty Rulings, Roman Laws or any Governor Rulings.

SOURCE OF INFORMATION

Guidance of the Holy Spirit, King James Version Bible, Archaeological Study Bible and Maxwell Leadership Bible.

SECTION A: THE PROPHECY FULLLFILLED

Activity	Location	Reference	Result
Triumphal entry	Jerusalem	Mark 11:9-10	The people cried Hosanna
Clears the temple	Jerusalem	Matt. 21:12-14	People told God's house is a house of prayer.
Jesus questioned	Jerusalem	Mark 11:27	Questions asked:
			(1) What authority are you doing these things?
			(2) Who gave you this authority?

SECTION A CONTINUED: THE PROPHECY FULLFILLED

Activity	Location	Reference	Notes
Mary anoints Jesus	Bethany	Matt. 26:6-13	Expensive alabaster box of oil was used.
Passover preparation	Jerusalem	Matt. 26:17-20	Passover Commemorated
The Lord's Supper	Jerusalem	Matt. 26:20-21	Betrayal & Instructions discussed.
Mount of Olives & Prayer (Garden of Gethsemane)	Gethsemane	Matt. 26:36, 42, and 44	Jesus prayed here three times
Jesus arrested, trial, And Crucified	Calvary	Mark 15:25,38	Taken to Golgotha. Nailed to the cross.

SECTION B: PERSONS/AGENCIES CONTACTED ABOUT THE COMPLAINT

Person/Agency	Location	Date of Contact	Notes
Chief Priest, Pharisees	John 11:47	near time for Passover	Plotting to kill Jesus.
Judas Iscariot		Matt. 26:14-16	after anointed by Mary Identified Jesus to the guards.

SECTION C: PROCEDURE OF THE TRIAL

Person/Agency	Location	Notes
Jewish Council	John 5:18	A written authorization from Governor needed.
Roman Soldiers	Matt. 26:46-50	Jesus arrested with no evidence.
Annas	John 18:12-14	Preliminary Hearing: Jesus illegally taken in middle of night.
Caiphas	John 18:24	Preliminary Hearing: Illegally gathering information on Jesus.
False Witnesses	Mark 14:57-58	Cannot incriminate Jesus without witnesses.
Sanhedrin Council	Matt. 27:1-2	Approved this illegal hearing. To make the trial appear legal under grounds of "Blasphemy" in the eyes of Jews and "Treason" in the eyes of the Romans to get the Death Penalty.
Pilate	Luke 23:1-5	Pilate finds no fault. Jesus sent to Herod.
Herod Agrippa	Luke 23:9-12	Jesus is teased and mocked, then taken back to Pilate.
Pilate	Luke 23:13-25	Jesus is whipped. Then chosen between himself and Barabbas To go free. Barabbas chosen. Jesus sentenced to be crucified.

AN ENCOURAGEMENT IS WITHIN YOU - 3

SECTION D: LAWS THAT PROVE AN ILLEGAL TRIAL

1) Even before the trial began, it had been determined that Jesus must die (Mark 14:1). There was no "innocent before being proven guilty" approach.

2) False witnesses were sought to testify against Jesus (Matt. 26:59). Usually the religious leaders went through an elaborate system of screening witnesses to insure justice.

3) The trial was conducted at night (Luke 22:53-55), which was illegal according to the religious leaders' own laws.

4) No defense for Jesus was sought or allowed (Luke 22:67-71).

5) The High Priest placed Jesus under oath, but then incriminated him for what he said (Matt. 26:63-66).

SECTION E: JESUS LAST WORDS BEFORE CRUCIFIXCION

1) Eli, Eli, lama sabachthani (My God, My God, why hast thou forsaken me) – (Matt. 27:46).

2) Verily, I say unto thee, Today shalt thou be with me in paradise (Luke 23:43).

3) Father forgive them; for they know not what they do (Luke 23:34).

4) I thirst (John 19:28).

5) It is finished (John 19:30).

6) Father, into thy hands I commend my spirit (Luke 23:46).

SECTION F: DIRECT ACCESS

And behold the veil of the temple was ripped in twain from the top to the bottom (the barrier between God and the people was removed) – (Matt. 27:51).

AN ENCOURAGEMENT IS WITHIN YOU - 4

A servant of God knows God and His word for themselves. For God's word is heartfelt. Once you accept the Lord in your life, His spirit will abide in you. For when Jesus died, He said, "I will send unto you a comforter."

> But if the Spirit of him that raised up Jesus from the dead dwell in you, he that raised up Christ from the dead shall also quicken your mortal bodies by his Spirit that dwelleth in you. (Rom. 8:11 KJV)

God had a plan for our life, before we even thought about what we wanted to do with our life.

> Ye have not chosen me, but I have chosen you, and ordained you, that ye should go and bring forth fruit, and that your fruit should remain: that whatsoever ye shall ask of the Father in my name, he may give it you. (John 15:1.6)

Jesus voluntarily chose to lay down His life for us. No man took His life. In return, He asks us to believe (John 3:16, 20:31) we are saved through faith (Rom.1:17). Once you are saved, we are sealed with the Holy Spirit (Eph.1:13).

Please, make a choice to LIVE your life for Christ and look toward the encourager within you to assist when making decisions, needing encouragement, and sometimes just for peace.

Think and discuss.

1. How God loves you (Remember all things are of God);

2. How Jesus loves you (Remember he died for you);

3. How the Holy Spirit loves you (Remember he guides you);

4. How much you love God's creation (people, no matter what nationality);

5. How much you love God the Father, God the Son, and God the Holy Spirit?

Appendices
Work in Progress Notes

Date: _____

Resolved Date: _____

Challenge I am facing.

_____

Three ways I want to handle this situation.

1. _____

2. _____

3. _____

Three ways I could handle this situation.

1. _____

2. _____

3. _____

How I handled this situation.

_____

_____

_____

_____

This was

Positive _____

Negative _____

Not Sure _____

No Comments _____

Date: _____

Resolved Date: _____

Challenge I am facing.

_____

Three ways I want to handle this situation.

1. _____

2. _____

3. _____

Three ways I could handle this situation.

1. _____

2. _____

3. _____

How I handled this situation.

_____

This was

Positive _____

Negative _____

Not Sure _____

No Comments _____

Date: _____

Resolved Date: _____

Challenge I am facing.

_____

Three ways I want to handle this situation.

1. _____

2. _____

3. _____

Three ways I could handle this situation.

1. _____

2. _____

3. _____

How I handled this situation.

_____

This was

Positive _____

Negative _____

Not Sure _____

No Comments _____

Date: _____

Resolved Date: _____

Challenge I am facing.

_____

Three ways I want to handle this situation.

1. _____

2. _____

3. _____

Three ways I could handle this situation.

1. _____

2. _____

3. _____

How I handled this situation.

_____

This was

Positive _____

Negative _____

Not Sure _____

No Comments _____

Date: _____

Resolved Date: _____

Challenge I am facing.

_____

Three ways I want to handle this situation.

1. _____

2. _____

3. _____

Three ways I could handle this situation.

1. _____

2. _____

3. _____

How I handled this situation.

_____

This was

Positive _____

Negative _____

Not Sure _____

No Comments _____

Date: _____

Resolved Date: _____

Challenge I am facing.

_____

Three ways I want to handle this situation.

1. _____

2. _____

3. _____

Three ways I could handle this situation.

1. _____

2. _____

3. _____

How I handled this situation.

_____

This was

Positive _____

Negative _____

Not Sure _____

No Comments _____

Date: _____

Resolved Date: _____

Challenge I am facing.

_____

Three ways I want to handle this situation.

1. _____

2. _____

3. _____

Three ways I could handle this situation.

1. _____

2. _____

3. _____

How I handled this situation.

_____

This was

Positive _____

Negative _____

Not Sure _____

No Comments _____

Date: _____

Resolved Date: _____

Challenge I am facing.

_____

Three ways I want to handle this situation.

1. _____

2. _____

3. _____

Three ways I could handle this situation.

1. _____

2. _____

3. _____

How I handled this situation.

_____

This was

Positive _____

Negative _____

Not Sure _____

No Comments _____

Date: _____

Resolved Date: _____

Challenge I am facing.

_____

Three ways I want to handle this situation.

1. _____

2. _____

3. _____

Three ways I could handle this situation.

1. _____

2. _____

3. _____

How I handled this situation.

_____

This was

Positive _____

Negative _____

Not Sure _____

No Comments _____

Date: _____

Resolved Date: _____

Challenge I am facing.

_____

Three ways I want to handle this situation.

1. _____

2. _____

3. _____

Three ways I could handle this situation.

1. _____

2. _____

3. _____

How I handled this situation.

_____

This was

Positive _____

Negative _____

Not Sure _____

No Comments _____

Date: _____

Resolved Date: _____

Challenge I am facing.

_____

Three ways I want to handle this situation.

1. _____

2. _____

3. _____

Three ways I could handle this situation.

1. _____

2. _____

3. _____

How I handled this situation.

_____

This was

Positive _____

Negative _____

Not Sure _____

No Comments _____

Below are words of encouragement that were written to me at "Meet and Greet Your Author Day." Thank you to each person for the time taken to encourage me through prayer, advice, laughter, and through opportunities to speak and teach at various workshops, seminars, conferences etc.

These words are very special to me. Take a moment and read these encouraging words.

An Encourager Is Within You, written by Deborah Hamm, is an insightful study guide that allows you to look deep within and examine yourself and motives that might be hindering you as a Christian.

This book is an excellent format for a woman's bible study. Deborah states in her bookß, "Although, each Christian is to help and encourage each other, the encourager with the most impact should be the encourager within you". Through the eyes of Tatiana, a diva who appears to have everything and Grace, a sweet little silver haired senior citizen, we are able to see bits and pieces of ourselves. Tatiana gains personal insight and clarity from Grace's spiritual based wisdom. In this book we are encouraged to" Be Real and Stop Pretending", "Accepting is Only One Step", "Who Has Your Attention?" and "Impossibility to Man, Possibility to God" to list just a few of the chapters.

After reading, Deborah Hamm's book and the leading of the Holy Spirit, you may find many burdens lifted and you just might have a brand new lease on life.

Beatrice Toney Bailey,
Professional Speaker,
TV Host and Author of,
Farewell, My Friend.

****

"Brilliance of captivating and intriguing relevance that is within us and told without, saying a word."

Mimi B.

God will Keep you in
Perfect Peace Whose
Whose mind is Stayed
On thee. Donna Stalberetti

Auntie, Everything you do inspires me to
do better! congrats on the Book &
may God continue to bless you! ☺ Zack

Sister Deborah, you know that you are a
tremendous blessing to me and all who
know you. May God continue to bless and
keep you and use you to further His
agenda. God bless you, beautiful woman
of God! Love your sis Bridgette Bell

Sister Sister, Thank you for your
encouragement, your wisdom and
your work with my son. God
bless you always ❤ Lisa

Sister Sharon I'm excited about
your book and what God is
doing in your life. You are awesome!
R. Valdry

Listen Mrs. Hamm I mean mom. I have loved you since the first time you said the ham joke. You have been with me since then encouraging me & telling me that I can do anything. I jest wish to tell go on Keep sharing. Be the light that you are - George Borges

God bless you Keep on teaching & sveen

Debra I love you so much I'm proud of you
Dellune

Hey Coo's
Thank You for All you do And your dedication
Thomas Dillard

Thank God for you you speak nothing but wisdom that I am touched by
Barbara Hester

Sister Hamm

Glorious Woman of God. Please please, please Keep God the head of your life. You are such an inspiration to us all. On behalf of Ascension - We love you - Keep dancing! Love
518. Melinda

Dear Sister Hanna
Thank you for being so
encouraging & loving to
us as a family and especially
to my daughter.
Love
Phillis

May God continue to Bless you
Continue to let Him use you - Bro. Carl Brown

May we continue to encourage you in
your Devotion to God first and to your
authority second. Bless you in all your efforts
Nancy Hicks

For my Sister (twin) in Christ
I love you & thank you for
being such a special friend!
Thank you for all of your
support teachings & encouragement!
your (twin) Sister!
April

Dear Debra,
May God continue to bless your
ministry - Tammy

Dear Ms Debbie
   I just praise God for you.
You are so Awesome in
everything you do. Thank
you for being a great
Mentor. I love you
and wish you the best
in everything you do.
   Cha-La   Ms. Loreene

Debra,
God has blessed you dearly,
Remember to keep him in your
life and he continue to bless
he takes us through but there's
light at the end of the tunnel.
We love you unconditionally.
Jerry DeVonne Moore
Dad - Brooks Hillian, SR.

Dear Sis Debra,
It is a blessing to know a
person who's life is being
used by God. Please continue
to bring the word forth for
the people of God thru your writing
Blessing
Theresa Orley

Dear Sis. Debra

I thank God for you!
I thank God for your ministry
I thank God for allowing you
to be you - the person that He called
you to be. Praise God
Sis Sheryl Counter

Dear Sis Debra,

You are a wonderful spirit,
encouraging, and full of
motivation. Thank you for
being obedient to the Spirit
to allow you to share your
gift. Love,
Sis Teresa Green

Sister Debra,

Its so wonderful to be associated with such a Godly Woman.

Bro. Kip Bins Sr